First-Year Sobriety

First-Year Sobriety

When All That Changes Is Everything

GUY KETTELHACK

HAZELDEN

Hazelden
Center City, Minnesota 55012-0176
1-800-328-0094 (Toll-free U.S., Canada, and the Virgin Islands)
1-651-213-4590 (Fax)
www.hazelden.org

Library of Congress Cataloging-in-Publication Data

Kettelhack, Guy.
    First-year sobriety : when all that changes is everything / Guy
Kettelhack.
        p.   cm.
    Originally published: 1st ed. San Francisco : HarperSanFrancisco,
© 1992 (Harper sobriety series ; v. 1).
    ISBN 13: 978-1-56838-230-2

    1. Alcoholics—Rehabilitation—United States—Case studies.
I. Title.
[HV5279.K48   1998]
362.292'86—dc21   98–28451
                                                                CIP

2016 15 14   / 17 16 15

Book design by Will H. Powers
Cover design by David Spohn
Typesetting by Stanton Publication Services, Inc.

Editor's note
The first-person stories in this book accurately reflect the feelings,
experiences, and circumstances expressed by recovering individuals, but
all names, locations, and identifying details have been changed.

Contents

Author's Note

I'm a recovering alcoholic and a writer who has grappled for some time with how to express what "recovery" means. The triumph and beauty of recovery from addiction is, to me, endlessly fascinating. Seeking to understand what goes on in recovery seems to me to be exploring what it means to become fully human.

So far, the best way I've found to convey the miraculous consciousness I find in recovery is simply to report what I hear from other recovering people. I've tried to be a kind of journalistic sponge, soaking up information, attempting to pass it on with as little interference as possible. This approach brings me one especially happy dividend: The sponge, as it soaks up information about recovery, ends up profiting as much as anyone else. The adventure of sobriety chronicled in this and other books I've done about recovery applies to *me* too. The bottom line is that I feel like a wide-eyed kid listening to what other people tell me about their recovery—as excited and grateful to have been helped by their experience, strength, and hope as I hope you will be, too, reading about it in these pages. The spirit of this book can be expressed simply: *We're all in this together.*

What I hope to do here is to offer you, via the voices and insights of hundreds of recovering alcoholics and drug addicts I've listened to across the country, a rich sense of the strange, sometimes frightening, usually baffling, but ultimately wonderful adventure sobriety can mean. Whatever year, month, day, hour, or moment of sobriety you may be facing right now, you will, I hope, find strong evidence herein that you can get through it in full consciousness: You don't have to pick up a drug or a drink. That's the main testament of the people whose stories you'll read here and the main message of hope. It's our experience that life lived consciously pretty much always beats the life lived blindly. I hope you'll let the people in this book show you how and why, one day at a time, we've found that to be true.

Acknowledgments

Every one of the recovering men and women whose stories are chronicled in this series is owed a debt of gratitude I cannot ever hope to repay, except, perhaps, by passing on their message—that we can all live more fully, joyfully, and consciously, no matter what our "stage" of sobriety—to as wide an audience as possible. I am thankful to them, and to you, for teaching me that we can all live sober and satisfying lives.

First-Year Sobriety

Introduction

"Mama Never Told Me it Would Be Like This"

Lori rubs her brow and frowns.

"This isn't how it was supposed to be," she says. "When I was little, my mother told me when I grew up I'd get married, like her, and have kids, like her, and live happily ever after." She looks out the window thoughtfully. "She never told me I'd move from city to city, live alone or with men I barely knew, get so depressed I'd want to kill myself. She never told me I'd be an alcoholic. And now, God help me," she says with a look of complete bafflement, "a *recovering* alcoholic."

The phrase "Mama never told me it would be like this" had a lot of meaning to Lori. She'd lettered it into a sign and tacked it up in her kitchen where she knew she'd be sure to see it every day. It reminded her, she said, "how unpredictable life is, and how adaptable I have to be to face life. I need to see something that will take away any expectations I might have about how I'm going to feel during the day. To remind me that the only thing I'm guaranteed is I won't get drunk if I don't drink." She laughs. "Do I sound too much like Little Miss AA? I hate it when I sound like I'm spouting the party line." She pauses and looks out the window again. "Oh, hell," she says, finally. "The truth is, I don't have the slightest idea what's happening to me. All I know is I've never felt this way before. My sponsor says that alcoholics who drink are like plants that manage to get along on almost no sun and water. When we stop drinking, and we start getting sun and water, it's a shock. We've forgotten what growth feels like—and here we are, *growing* all of a sudden. That's supposedly why I feel this way. I'm not used to living life like this. Consciously. Head on.

"My sponsor also says—I seem to be starting more and more sentences that way!—that all I've got to do is stop drinking and go to AA meetings every day to let this natural growth happen. She says I don't have to think about it, or force my will on anything. Just don't drink, and go to meetings." Lori groans softly. "Usually I take it on faith. I mean, all I know is that everything feels new and pretty uncomfortable. Sometimes I just zonk out, stare out the window and get lost in how bright everything looks. Sometimes I feel so much pain—then, out of nowhere, this amazing feeling of well-being, even joy." Lori lets out a baffled sigh. "God knows where all this will take me. For now, I'm just hanging in there, letting life happen . . . and making a day-to-day pact with myself not to drink while it does."

Lori's feelings of newness and confusion in sobriety may strike familiar chords in you. Or perhaps they don't. Things probably feel different for you than they used to, but possibly in a different way from what Lori describes. Which brings us to what may be the only universal statement we can make about the onset of sobriety: It's not the same for everyone.

However, if sobriety is such a singular experience, how can we say anything in a book that speaks to everyone? Can Lori's message, "Mama never told me it would be like this," be made into a welcome mat? Something that invites all of us in?

It's true that your experience of your first day or seven days or three weeks or ninety days or four or six months or a year of sobriety will be your own. Nobody can quite understand what it's like for you to get through life without picking up a drug or a drink. You may realize from day one of sobriety that what's happening to you is something very special and private, a gift that peculiarly fits your soul, a gift that somehow slipped into you in the most intimate and particular way (if you feel it to be a gift at all: some people don't, at least not right off). How could anyone besides you understand what this feels like, what you're going through?

The people you'll meet in these pages all have this feeling of specialness, and they all deserve to have it. Their route to sobriety is, in some crucial ways, uniquely their own: They have all experienced life without drinking or drugging in ways peculiar to each of them. Not that there aren't universals; we'll see throughout this book that there are many feelings that do seem to unite recovering people, samenesses that are the more striking for the diversity they come out of. But we generalize about recovering people at our peril. For example, some people seem to ascend almost immediately to what people in Twelve Step programs call "a pink cloud"; things just get amazingly, wonderfully better, right from the start! Other people discover resentments, anger, or depression with a ferocity that may frighten others who don't feel those things; sobriety is tough for these guys, and they don't understand what the "happy, joyous, and free" stuff is all about. Others feel like they're stumbling around, rubbing their eyes after a Rip Van Winkle–length coma. "Where the hell am I?" one newly recovering alcoholic asks.

Others still feel differently. Some people make the transition to sobriety more easily than others, with greater or lesser degrees of comfort and clarity. All of which brings us to the first premise of this book, which is also a premise of the volumes in this series about the first three years in sobriety: *There is no "right" or "wrong" way to feel in sobriety.* Maybe this relieves you: "You mean, *any* way I feel is okay?" But you might just as easily have a different reaction. The idea that any way they feel is okay scares some people out of their wits. "Tell me what to expect!"

they say. "I can't stand this uncharted territory. What am I supposed to be feeling? Give me some rules!"

Fortunately or unfortunately, there don't appear to be any rules about feelings in sobriety. As you may already know from your own experience in these first days or months of your first year, what we've said is true: People respond differently; sobriety colors our lives in very individual ways. But you may also have begun to get the clue that there are *suggestions* that can be worth following, suggestions that can make our paths in sobriety easier and that seem to work for all of us, no matter how different we are as individuals. These suggestions are worth looking at carefully because they appear to have worked, over time, for so many people. They come from the real experience of other recovering addicts and alcoholics who have managed to stay sober before us, experience that's given rise perhaps most popularly and effectively to the Twelve Step programs of AA and NA and other A's based on Twelve Step principles and traditions.

Luckily, there's a good deal of literature available about all this—books and pamphlets that offer some very specific tips about the nuts and bolts of staying sober, such as ways of doing the Twelve Steps and of dealing with a wide range of other issues in sober living. (See Suggested Reading at the back of this book for some recommendations.) This book, however, is a little different. We're not going to give you a step-by-step How to Live Sober guide. Our task is to give you something a little less quantifiable, but, we think, just as necessary and healing.

What this book will give you is voices. Many voices. Voices of people who, like you, are struggling in the often baffling territory of their first year of trying to live without drinking or drugging. People who, like you, are alternately amazed, appalled, delighted, depressed, illuminated, elated, disturbed, or simply thrown by their first days, weeks, and months of sobriety. These voices are male and female, straight and gay, young and old, rich and poor. What unites them is that they're all in the process of giving life without alcohol and drugs a chance. Something else unites them, too, in what they have to offer us: an overarching message of hope.

Whether you're feeling up or down, the people in this book tell us, *you can get through it without picking up a drink or taking a drug.* If you've managed to do that, you're the greatest success in the world. Nothing is better than what you've done simply by getting through the day without picking up. That's our second premise and the bottom-line definition of success that we use in this book: *You're a success if you've managed not to pick up today.* In fact, every day you manage to resist the urge to pick up, you deserve all the congratulations and encouragement in the world.

Does this mean you're not a success if you slip? In these pages you'll meet a number of people who have had what they consider one or more false starts in sobriety, people who may have managed to amass some time in recovery but ended up being unable to sustain it. Are they failures? No. Certainly they don't consider *themselves* failures, even if they couldn't stick with sobriety at first. They realize, from hard experience, that "it takes what it takes" to fully wake up to the power of their addictions, and to the potential joys and rewards of learning ways to live without allowing those addictions to run—and ruin—their lives.

Nobody said sobriety was easy. It isn't the role of this book to judge anybody who drinks or doesn't drink, takes drugs or doesn't. All we'd like to suggest clearly at the outset is that, if you have come to acknowledge that you are addicted and you manage, through whatever means, to stay away from the substance or behavior you're addicted to, you're participating in a miracle. You're experiencing the basic bedrock success we hold as the most precious thing we've experienced in our own lives as recovering addicts and alcoholics.

A third premise: While this isn't a Twelve Step recovery guide, this is a book primarily about Twelve Step recovery. The men and women you'll meet in these pages have all found direction and support and hope in Twelve Step programs. This isn't to say you won't get something out of this book if you're still in the "undecided" category regarding AA or NA or any of the other A's. Sobriety is sobriety, no matter how you achieve it—assuming, that is, it's true psychological and spiritual sobriety, and not mere abstinence from drugs and alcohol. However, we do hold a Twelve Step bias—and for a simple reason. From the evidence of the huge number of people whose voices fill these pages, Twelve Step programs *work*. While no one associated with this book is an AA spokesperson (which is in any case an impossibility—by its own definition AA can have no spokespeople), the "experience, strength, and hope" of people in Twelve Step programs inform the tone of *First-Year Sobriety* and largely provide its content.

What we hope is that these pages will speak to you the way a Twelve Step meeting does. In fact, that's a good way to think of this book. Put it in your pocket, bag, purse, briefcase, or backpack and take it out when you need a meeting and can't get to one. Some voices may delight you, others may infuriate you, others may seem familiar, still others may sound as if they come from another planet. (Just like a regular Twelve Step meeting!) You may want to laugh or cry or think or maybe even snooze a little. Just as there's no "right" or "wrong" way to experience sobriety, there's no right or wrong way to experience a Twelve Step meeting, or this book.

All we ask is that you give the people you'll meet here a chance to speak to you, and yourself the chance of being helped and healed. Healing, in the experience of the people in this book, seems to happen most effectively and satisfyingly when you realize a simple fact: *You're not alone.* If you're going through your first days or weeks or months of sobriety, it will almost certainly help to hear and realize that.

But isn't this contradictory? What about everything we said earlier about how unique each of is?

Sure, nobody is exactly like you. But nobody is completely different from you either. You can call that our fourth premise, if you'd like. Twelve Step programs suggest that you "identify, not compare," because it's been the experience of people who have achieved sobriety in Twelve Step programs that you can get something helpful from anyone who speaks in recovery, however different his or her circumstances may be from your own. There do seem to be some clear common denominators in the emotional realm: Our *feelings* always seem to connect us, even when the particulars of our experiences may not.

As you'll also see in this book, there are no timetables in recovery. Some people "get" certain intuitions or insights that other people don't. The fact is, some people battle much fiercer demons in sobriety than others. We all drag different baggage into sobriety; some bags are easier to unload than others. Again, while this is a book about the first year of sobriety, you won't find any "right" or "wrong" way to accomplish that first year. True, as we've said, evidence from the people in this book indicates that there do seem to be a few ballpark universals, challenges we all seem to end up facing: learning to break through loneliness and isolation and fear; finding ways to deal with anger and depression and resentment; learning how to tolerate a new and sometimes overwhelming happiness (sometimes joy can be as hard to deal with in sobriety as misery!). A certain identifiable broad territory of discovery does seem to make itself felt in the first year. But we emphasize "broad." There's room for every human experience here. Including yours.

But enough premises. Let's get to some of what "Mama never told you it would be like." And feel free, imaginatively, to join the voices here: Add your own story to the stories you'll find in this book.

There is a way back from hell. Join us in charting it.

one

When All That Changes Is Everything:
The First Ninety Days

Here are four brief stories about a variety of people in the first stages of their recovery. You'll go first to a large urban hospital and meet a group of alcoholics and addicts in "detox," men and women used to hearing themselves called "hard cases." Then you'll meet Susan, a soft-spoken young woman in the Midwest who's had a hard time convincing her family (and sometimes herself) that she is an alcoholic. Next you'll meet Pablo, a streetwise twenty-year-old man from Detroit who's spent his life trying to be Superman. And Charles, a seventy-year-old newly sober gentleman from Boston who often finds himself feeling like a child.

As different as these people may seem from one another, you may also get a glimmer of what unites them. And what may apply to you.

We're in a brightly lit room in a New York hospital. About twenty-five people, more men than women, dressed in hospital-issued blue pajamas, sit around two long fold-out dining tables that have been pushed together. Miguel breaks the silence.

"This place *sucks*," he says. A tough-looking guy in his mid-thirties, Miguel is full of submerged energy, like a volcano waiting to blow. He stares down at his hands clenched in his lap. His voice is so quiet he can barely be heard, but the people around the table who are listening (not everyone is) seem to be catching it. "I hate this place. I can't stand it. I want to run out of here every minute. I feel like I'm gonna *explode* if I don't get out of here." His glowering eyes lift to scan the room, then drop back down to his hands. "What the *hell* good is hanging around you bozos supposed to be doing for me?"

Sam, a black man of greater bulk than Miguel but with a far more easygoing manner, responds, "Hey man. Stick around to play Monopoly with me. You're the only guy here as good as me at it."

People laugh. Miguel is caught off guard. He lets out a long low *whoosh* of air, which seems to calm him down a little.

"I know what Miguel means," says Theresa, a dark woman who tends to take charge of these sessions. "This sobriety is a bitch. I mean, what did we always do before? We got high. That was how we handled anything and everything. My feelings make me wanna bust out of my skin, too, sometimes. Sometimes all I wanna do is go out and cop and get high." Theresa frowns, then pounds the table with her right fist, which startles two or three men nodding off at the end of the table to her left. They look up at her in surprise.

"But it doesn't frigging *work* anymore," she continues, "and we don't know what the hell else to *do*. So we're here to learn something. I mean, we're not here on vacation, man. Right?" A chorus of "Rights." "Jesus!" Theresa starts to laugh, turning again to Miguel. "I mean—*look* at you, man! I saw you when you were out there. You were a mess. I couldn't understand a word you said, and now here we are, sitting around like all this was normal, talking like regular people. *Something* the hell is goin' on here. It's better than it used to be. Stick around for it, man." She smiles at Miguel again, softens her voice. "Stick around."

An old man named Joseph looks down with watery blue eyes

at his spotless pajama shirt and then looks up, bewildered. "I'm even *clean*," he says, mostly to himself, baffled that anything like that could have happened.

Jorge begins to rock back and forth in his chair. Theresa is annoyed. "Stop that, man! You like a crazy person!" These "group sessions" tend to make Theresa edgy, and she doesn't like it when anyone acts up. But Jorge won't stop rocking back and forth. Everyone in the room looks at him, some people out of boredom (a number of people in here dread "Group" more than anything else they've got to sit through in detox), some people out of curiosity. A man of indeterminate years—maybe forty-five, maybe sixty—Jorge has never opened his mouth in the whole two weeks he's been here. He rocks back and forth more vigorously now, his face a frown of concentration. "What the hell you doing?" Theresa is getting angry.

Jorge opens his mouth and makes a sound. Finally, the people around him hear what he's saying. "My name is Jor-ge"—he draws out the sounds "Hooor-haaay" as if testing his voice, jaws, tongue to see if they work. With a further effort of concentration, he manages, "and—I—am—an—alco—holic."

Those people who are paying attention suddenly applaud. Even the bored ones look at Jorge and clap their hands. They know something special has happened, even if they aren't sure exactly what. Theresa smiles and gets up out of her chair to hug Jorge, who doesn't smile, but stops rocking in his chair.

Susan sits by the bay window of her living room, her troubled look at odds with the peacefulness of the rolling Illinois landscape.

"I think the most unnerving thing," she says, "is that so many people never thought I had a problem with drinking. They just don't believe I'm an alcoholic. Sometimes I think even people in AA look at me as if I don't belong. I imagine everyone thinking, 'What's *she* doing here?'" Susan pauses for a moment, looks out the window. "Sometimes this scares me. I mean, maybe I'm

not an alcoholic. That's what it seems everyone wants me to believe. It's certainly what my mother said when I told her. 'Oh,
Susan,' she said, 'you're always making problems for yourself.
No one from our family ever had a drinking problem. You're just
blowing it out of proportion.'"

Any suggestion of crisis or a negative feeling, Susan says, had
always been pushed down, minimized, never talked about in her
family. "My dad is a retired army officer," Susan continues. "The
fact that we're black—and that he had a black family in the
midst of the all-white midwestern town we lived in—made him
feel we all had to try harder. Be an example or something. We
weren't allowed to fight, express anger, sadness—act in any way
other than what he decided was 'normal.'"

Susan heaves a big sigh. "So I became the best little girl in the
world. The best little girl grew up, got good grades, did everything right. And felt less and less human with every passing year.
Less and less like there was any possibility of finding out who
I really was, much less being it." Right after college, Susan married a "respectable" man going through medical school—"someone my father might have picked for me"—and tried hard to
become a model wife and later, after one, then two, then three
kids ("My husband's religious background makes him shun birth
control—sometimes I think he wants me to populate the
world"), a model mother. She discovered, on some evenings out
with her husband's doctor friends and their wives, that she could
be a model drinker too.

"It was amazing what a few glasses of wine could do," Susan
says. "It was like it didn't take so much energy and willpower
anymore to be nice, charming, say all the right things. Wine was
a miracle; a few glasses and I was all those things without trying.
And I was a *nice* drinker. Funny, open, charming. Something in
me released—relaxed. It wasn't such a chore anymore to be alive."

Susan looks out the window again. "I never drank more than
three, maybe four glasses of wine at a time," she says. "I mean,

I wasn't out of control. The idea that I might have a *problem* with drinking never occurred to me. And if anyone had suggested I was an alcoholic, I would have questioned their sanity. Alcoholics were people who slept in the gutter. I was doing just fine."

Certainly the outer parts of Susan's life continued to appear "fine." "I don't have much of a war story, really," she says. "It's enough to say that wine was so terrific at dinner that I figured, why wouldn't it be just as terrific at lunch? Or in the middle of the afternoon? Or after my husband left in the morning for the hospital, the two littlest kids were taking their naps, and my oldest was off in nursery school? These were just 'time out' periods for me, I thought. And nobody but me had to know about them. Afterwards, a few swigs of mouthwash and I was okay, good as new. . . ."

Susan eventually realized she wasn't okay, not because anything terrible happened—"It's a miracle that something terrible *didn't* happen to one of the kids, with me half-drunk all day"—but because of an inner despair that the wine couldn't seem to touch anymore. "After a few years, drinking wasn't making me feel better. It was deepening my depression, not lifting it. I started to feel suicidal. Something was terribly, terribly wrong with me, and I couldn't imagine what it was." Susan made a secret appointment with a therapist she'd overheard one of the neighbors talk about, a woman who turned out to be an alcoholism counselor. "Talk about a Higher Power," Susan says, smiling for the first time. "That was about a month ago."

Ever the obedient little girl, Susan followed the therapist's suggestion that she try AA in conjunction with therapy. "At first, I was appalled by everyone baring their feelings so publicly—in front of strangers! But then, I don't know, after a week or so of meetings, something started to release in me." Her brow furrows. "I guess I wouldn't have kept this up if I weren't ready for it. But I'm still pretty baffled by what's happening to me, what I'm feeling. Strangely, I don't miss drinking all that much now.

What's throwing me is what's happening to me inside—feelings are starting to come up I never knew were there."

Susan sighs. "Nobody in my family has a clue what's going on. My husband treats me like I'm some good-natured but confused little girl. He thinks it's nice that I go to AA for 'support,' but he's convinced this is just a passing phase and I'll snap out of it. He couldn't possibly bring himself to think he'd married an *alcoholic*. As he keeps telling me, he's never seen me drunk. I'm too much of a lady for that. . . ."

Susan smiles again. "You know why I think I keep going to AA? Not only because I know that drinking was beginning to worsen my depression, but because it gives me people to talk to, to listen to. People who keep telling me I'll learn who I really am if I just 'keep coming back.' What an amazing idea—that I might actually have a self independent of my family, my parents, my husband, the narrow goody-two-shoes life I've always had! I feel like a sneak, sometimes." She laughs. "All the people who are so patronizing to me in life—'Oh, isn't it nice that she has a group of friends to talk to!'—don't realize how revolutionary this may all turn out to be. Wait till they see the *real* me." Susan laughs again. "Whoever that is."

"I've got some idea that when I hit ninety days I'll get a revelation," she continues. "God will suddenly boom down from the clouds at me and let me know: '*This* is who you are.' And then I'll start being whoever that is. But my recovering friends tell me that probably won't happen. Whatever road I'm on is longer and stranger than I think it is. *Better*, too, they keep saying.

"Well," Susan says as she looks out the window again, "I'll have to see for myself."

Pablo sits sullenly in his chair.

"Who the hell decided that 'ninety days' was the magic number?" he says. "I mean, why not sixty-four days or eighty-seven days or one hundred and sixteen days?"

Pablo is long, lean, and about twenty years old. His hair, dyed a stark "neo" black, is cropped off about mid-skull, shaven from there down his neck. Three gleaming silver studs adorn his left earlobe. Taut with energy, he's not someone who's happy about having to sit still. "This Twelve Step shit gets me, sometimes," he says. "Those *slogans*—it's like frigging first grade." Pablo continues in a whiny falsetto, wagging his finger like a schoolteacher: "Easy Does It—But *Do It!*" His eyes roll up and he groans.

"And Christ, all this *God* shit. I'm supposed to turn my life over to *who?!*" He groans again. "Are they crazy or what?" Pablo has been in and out of "the rooms" a half dozen times. "Never made it past thirty days," he used to say proudly. But he's got seventy-five days now, a record, and he's not able to hide a slight tone of amazement: "Okay, it's pretty bizarre that I'm off my usual shit for this long," he says softly. "I mean I was mainlining at thirteen, a fuckin' heroin addict all my life. Pot was like Coca-Cola to me—something you sucked up as a little kid. And, hell, booze—getting drunk was just something you did, like breathe."

Pablo grew up and still lives in one of the poorest and most dangerous neighborhoods of Detroit. "I was a goddamn little Superman," he says. "Nothing I wouldn't do." High on any number of drugs, Pablo would jump from five- or six-story buildings onto moving buses, trucks, and cars, "scaring the shit out of the passengers"—somehow, miraculously, without ever getting hurt. He was a master thief and a persuasive panhandler. He was also something of a lady-killer. "Had a rep," Pablo says, beaming, now. "Had some ladies woulda *paid* me for it, you wanna know the truth."

But here he is now, off drugs and booze for seventy-five days. What's it like for him?

For a moment, his eyes soften a little and it looks as if he'll answer. But this isn't territory he's used to, and he doesn't like talking about it. "I don't know," he says. However, the next day, his seventy-sixth without drugs or booze, he decides to let out something of what sobriety is beginning to mean to him.

"It's not like I was *scared* or anything," he says. "It's just—I don't know—it just wasn't the same anymore. I kept doing stuff and not getting really zonked out like I used to. It's like there was this part of me I couldn't *get* to anymore. I couldn't put out the light." He pauses, looks down at his hands, curls them into fists

"You know, I have this dream sometimes. I'm in the ring, pounding and pounding away at some chump. . . ." He throws a few quick jabs and uppercuts into the air. "Once I almost joined a boxing gym, thought I'd go pro, you know? I'm a pretty tough mutha." His eyes flash for a moment, then grow distant. "Anyways, so, this dream . . . There I am trying to knock this guy out, and he's still standing there, getting the shit beat out of him, but he doesn't go down. No matter how hard I hit the guy, his head flips back, the sweat flies, my arms are getting so friggin' tired, and the guy's still standing. His eyes are open, and I take a good look at him still standing there and I get this freaked-out idea that, you know, he's me. I mean, he doesn't really look like me, but it doesn't matter. Somehow I know he's me anyway."

Pablo's defenses gather; the wall shoots back up again for a moment. "Don't, like, do any shrink shit about this, huh? It's just some crazy stupid dream. Doesn't mean anything." He looks back down at his hands, now, as his fists slowly relax into open palms. "Except it does mean something, I guess," he says quietly. The wall recedes and he opens up a little. "I get so fed up sometimes. So damned tired. I keep thinking there's gotta be some other way, you know? I look around at other guys, even guys older than me, and I feel like I'm older than them sometimes. Yeah, I know, I'm supposed to be twenty, but sometimes I feel like I'm a hundred. I'm tired of this shit." He looks up. "It's like, if the guy can't get knocked out, maybe it's time for him to get out of the ring. Maybe the guy even wants to."

Suddenly his eyes flash again, his energy roars up—time for a mood change. "So, hey, man—back to first grade! And I got

....*seventy-six days.*" He smiles, a softer light in his eyes. "Never had that before."

Charles adjusts his tie and laughs a little.

"I don't know why this should pop into my mind," he says. "But I saw a comic strip this morning, something about a thirteen-year-old girl and her travails—you know, she's 'average,' not too pretty, has a bratty older brother, no boyfriend, she's exasperated by her parents, hates school, the usual stuff—and she's just had her first period. Pretty progressive little comic strip! Anyway, she's strutting around her messy room in the first two frames: 'No more Barbie dolls!' she says, 'no more stuffed animals, no more kid stuff—move over, Madonna, here I come!' That sort of thing. And then, in the last frame, she looks around at the wreckage of her room, all her dolls and teddy bears strewn across the floor, and a little bubble of thought appears over her head: '*Wait* a minute . . .'"

Charles's blue eyes are thoughtful, sad. "Here I am," he says after a moment, "nearly seventy years old, comfortable financially, supposedly all grown up—and I feel just like that thirteen-year-old girl. I miss my teddy bears, my cradle. I miss—" He clears his throat and assumes his more usual stance, that of a competent, elegant, well-turned out "older" man. But he can't entirely hide his sadness, his feelings of loss. "I miss alcohol—sometimes it can knock me over, how much I miss it. It's like my best friend died. Or I've been kicked out of the only home I ever knew. And now I've got to fend for myself, according to a God-knows-what new set of rules."

He rubs his hands together and frowns. "Who'd have thought ninety days of abstinence would do this to me—turn me into this frightened, vulnerable little child? God, it was never like this for me before. *I* was the one people thought had all the answers; *I* was the person who seemed to have it all together." Charles was a respected art historian and appraiser; his eye was one of the most trusted in the business. "I've always rather enjoyed the bowing and scraping I got, even from some of the better-known curators. I liked leaving the impression that my intuitions—not only about art but about life—were somehow inexpressibly subtle, omniscient. Even," Charles's eyes gleam, "godlike. I always *seemed* to be someone virtually untouchable. At least that's the image I assiduously—and frankly, quite successfully—managed to cultivate."

"Seemed" was, indeed, the operative word in his life, Charles says. "I knew, secretly, that I was never really who everyone thought I was. I had whole dark spaces in me I kept secret. Whole lives I lived when I drank that would have shocked my Martha's Vineyard friends. For one thing, being gay—I mean, I suppose nearly everyone in my life *knows*, but there's this sort of discretion about it: hostesses at dinner parties still provide me with 'eligible' partners. Most of whom," Charles says merrily, "are lesbian. But nobody knows the debauches I've been through drunk—the dark bars and parks and . . . well, the important point is that I'm finding ways to let some light and air in on all that now. I'm discovering I can actually begin to *talk* about those dark spaces—to complete strangers I wouldn't have dreamed would be in my life four months ago!" He shakes his head in disbelief.

"Sometimes I look around 'the rooms'—that's the generic term AA people use for meeting places, isn't it?—and I think, how extraordinarily well behaved everyone is! And how god-awful it would be if, somehow, through some weird science fiction quirk, we were all returned in an instant to the selves we were when we drank. The chairs thrown, the sulking, the yelling, the crying, the fights. . . . None of these people would have gotten along with each other for a minute! I wouldn't have given the time of day to seven-eighths of the people I now regularly spend hours with." Charles snorts an abrupt laugh. "Now I find myself baring my soul to them!"

"Them," Charles says, covers a good big territory. "Meetings in Boston are quite a cross section, I can tell you. And my sponsor, God help me, is a *plumber.*" Charles laughs. "A damned good one too. I use him regularly. Interesting phenomenon to have your sponsor fix your pipes. There's a metaphor there somewhere. . . ." Charles evidently feels the need to apologize for his "classism": "I know I'm a snob. You would be too, if you had the kind of blue-blood thrashing of an upbringing I had. But—well, things have changed."

Charles recounts an experience he had the previous morning, leaving his elegant building on one of the most exclusive streets of Boston's Beacon Hill.

"There's a vestibule in my building, the door to which is almost always locked, but which had been left open by some negligent tenant the night before. A little man, reeking of alcohol—his red puffy face tucked into his arm, his body in a heavily drugged fetal position—had camped out on the marble parquet floor. At first I was terrified. I'm not a young man, and I'm an awful coward. But this little creature was dead to the world. As I saw, drunk as he was, how little a threat he posed, I got terribly self-righteous. Did a mean, bellowing Orson Welles: 'Get the hell out of my building!'

"The little creature opened his eyes, painfully, slowly, and, God, I remembered all those hundreds, thousands of mornings when I felt exactly as I knew he felt then. This sudden softening came over me. This little, smelly, pathetic drunken man and I were the same. I found myself saying, 'I know how you feel. I've been there. I used to drink like you do.' The man looked up at me, slowly registering what I'd said, and I saw this indescribable sweetness in him—this *humanity.* He was no longer something to be discarded, which is, frankly, how I'd always seen homeless drunks before. He was—well, *me.*"

Charles's eyes mist for a moment, then clear. "Of course, like me, he was expert at psyching out and taking advantage of a soft touch. He'd evidently interpreted my expression of empathy as an invitation to stay—in any event, he still hadn't moved. I again told him to get out of the vestibule, but I sounded a little less like Orson Welles. And I understood something very clearly. I've never met an alcoholic, recovering or not, who didn't ache for escape—escape from the sense that he had to be something other than who he was. We all ache for someone to say, 'Just be yourself. You don't have to be anything you aren't.' All that drunk wanted was to be left alone. To be himself. In a funny way, that's what I realize I've always wanted too. It's just that I've discovered thirteen or fourteen vodka martinis a night aren't the way to meet that goal anymore."

Charles smiled. "I'm full of stories, aren't I? It's amazing to suddenly feel like I've got so much I want to *tell*. Ninety days of no booze, and look what's become of me. You can't shut me up." Charles looks bemused. "Who'd have thought it? Who'd have thought there was somebody here—somebody ready and willing to appear, after all these years, without the help of alcohol! I don't know how I acquired the ability to empathize with thirteen-year-old girls and homeless drunks, but thank God that I have. There's life beyond vodka. You couldn't have convinced me of *that* before. Not in a million years."

The people you've just met are basically random selections from an enormous and variegated garden: They constitute only a few of the blooms, some of which you may find exotic, others familiar, of newly planted, newly experienced sobriety. Different as they are from one another—and as they may be in certain respects from you—some of the feelings they have do seem to be similar. Being confused by the sudden onslaught of feelings in the new clarity of sobriety, feeling like a vulnerable child, mourning the escape alcohol or drugs meant even while accepting that the escape had become self-destructive (Pablo's dream made it clear that Pablo was the one getting beaten up), having a dawning sense of who you might be without alcohol and drugs, and, perhaps most of all, realizing that you don't have to go it alone—you *can* reach out for, and get, help: These are all themes common, if in different degrees, to everyone we've met, and to many, many other people in the first days of sobriety.

Our friends may be a bit *too* much alike in one respect, however. With the obvious exception of Jorge (in the hospital detox unit), they're all bursting with things to say, stories to tell about themselves. Not everyone working on his or her first ninety days of sobriety is quite this energetically articulate. As one sixty-six-year-old recovering man who'd just celebrated fifteen years of sobriety told me, "I never opened my mouth in the rooms for my first eight years; I kept going to meetings, but I was too frightened to actually speak in a meeting all that time." During those eight years he had gradually managed to open up one-on-one with a few recovering friends, and eventually to a sponsor he felt he could trust, but the idea of saying honestly how he felt in the relative public of a Twelve Step meeting was, for a long time, terrifying to him. "I wouldn't recommend my path of keeping silent to other recovering people," he said. "But it shows you that not all of us are ready to let it all out so soon."

Mary, a single mother (with a ten-year-old daughter) whose drinking and pill-taking stepped up dramatically when her husband left her—"one morning he woke up and decided he didn't love me anymore, and that was the last I saw of him"—has experienced a similar terror at AA meetings in her first month and a half of sobriety. "What do *I* know? I don't feel I *have* any 'experience, strength, and hope' to share yet. Everyone else sounds so good—like they've got all the answers. I just feel shell-shocked." Many other recovering alcoholics and drug addicts echo Mary, especially about her feelings of inadequacy.

Jim, a construction worker in Vermont, says, "I feel like such an ass now, when I think of what a big shot I tried to act like in the bars. Now I don't feel like I know anything. The AA meeting

I go to is small, everyone gets to know each other real well, and they won't let me shut up completely. But sometimes all I can do is say my name and that I'm an alcoholic, and rely on that trusty phrase 'I'll just listen today.'"

Physical Sobriety

The people you met earlier in the New York detox—Miguel, Sam, Theresa, Joseph, and Jorge—as well as Susan, Pablo, and Charles, haven't talked about another big reality that looms large for most, if not all, people in early sobriety: the *physical* differences they feel now that they're not drinking or drugging. The onset of physical sobriety sometimes leads to the biggest revelations, joys, and frustrations of anything people first experience when they put down alcohol and drugs.

We could spend a whole book on this topic alone. Recovering addicts and alcoholics rarely come into recovery in terrific shape: The sheer physical abuse to which many of us have subjected ourselves, often for years, can take any number of tolls. We're often war-torn—perhaps battling the HIV virus, or diabetes, liver damage, or intestinal problems—in addition to trying to adjust psychologically to life without drugs or alcohol. Issues about medication, such as whether or not we should take "mood-altering" drugs even when they're prescribed, all constitute a vast and complicated area. Simply how we *feel* about the physical changes we experience in sobriety can run the gamut from terrific to appalling.

We'll be touching on many of these dilemmas throughout the rest of this book. For now, it may help to focus on a few specifics, just to get us into the ballpark of what many recovering alcoholics and addicts first go through physically when they stop picking up. Let's just concentrate for the moment on two areas that seem to be especially absorbing (and exasperating) to most recovering people, especially in their first ninety days: sleep and food.

Sleeping Sober

A couple of people in their first ninety days illustrate two common experiences of sleep in early sobriety:

- "You know that Twelve Step acronym HALT, which is supposed to remind us not to get too hungry, angry, lonely, or tired?" asks Jonathan, a middle-aged businessman with five weeks of abstinence from drugs and alcohol. "I want to scream every time I hear that damned thing. I can't go to sleep. I keep trying, but I can't make it all the way through the night. It's like my body won't let me. It's so damned baffled that it didn't get its usual dose of cocaine or booze, it's like it's in revolt or something. 'Give me what I want!' it seems to be saying. And what it wants is to pass out, which is the only way it knew how to go to sleep before. And when I do sleep a little—God, the dreams! Such crazy dreams. Does anyone else grind their teeth like I do when they sleep? Sometimes I think I'll grind them down to the gums. Then, when I wake up, tossing and turning, I feel like I've got to hang on to the edges of my bed, just to keep from jumping out of my skin. There's some kind of weird physical detox going on, that's what it feels like, and, man, I'm exhausted." Jonathan snorts disgustedly. "And what does my sponsor say? 'Don't drink or drug, and go to meetings. Lack of sleep never killed anybody.'" He smiles evilly. "I know. I'll start calling him up in the middle of the night at five-minute intervals to make sure he doesn't get any sleep either!"
- Andrea has had a very different experience. "I'm a nurse," she says, "and I was easily able to get tranquilizers to knock myself out at night—mixing them, I thought, very carefully, with just the right amount of

wine. What I'd taught myself to do was pass out on cue, not sleep. But now—I can't tell you the difference. Not that it was easy getting used to sleeping sober at first. It wasn't. I probably went through a week and a half of purely physical withdrawal, and I was like a crazy woman. But then, I'll never forget it, I had one pure long night of real sleep. It felt so different. My dreams were different. On the rare occasions I could remember any dreams when I drank and drugged, they were so fantastically strange. I went to places like the moons of Jupiter, saw creatures with three heads, got caught in science fiction fantasies. In fact, I used to be proud of my dreams! 'Normal' people seemed to dream about their bosses and husbands and kids and stuff. I was dreaming about shooting around the solar system with a Cyclops on my left and a three-headed dog on my right. Now I realize I was having drugged hallucinations! In the two months I've been off drugs and booze, my dreams suddenly seem softer, more normal, more connected to my waking life. They're even sort of helpful; I can see how the sober mind sort of works things out in sleep. At least sometimes it feels that way."

Andrea closes her eyes and lets out a long, contented sigh, then continues, smiling. "I love going to sleep now. I even wonder sometimes if I'm not just replacing alcohol and drugs with sleep—if I'm not addicted to going to bed! But, no, it's different. I feel like I'm healing myself now. I get up feeling actually refreshed by sleep. It's unbelievable; that never happened before." Andrea laughs. "I'm also going to bed every night at about 9:00 P.M. God, I'm only thirty-five. You'd think I was eighty-five. But my sponsor says it takes real work being conscious all day. I can be forgiven if I get tired so early. And, hey, why not enjoy it!"

Jonathan's and Andrea's experiences represent two poles of newly sober people's experience with sleep. But other people have other experiences. Certainly there appear to be differences in adjustment between recovering drug addicts and recovering alcoholics. If you were a heavy cocaine user, you'll more than likely have a different experience (more like Jonathan's, on evidence) than if you were mainly battling alcohol or Valium. If you were used to medicating yourself, for example, with downers after spending the day on uppers (what Andrea calls "the Judy Garland grind"), it's not surprising if you're not able to fall blissfully off to sleep your first night or two off drugs. As Andrea puts it, "For years, I got used to hitting myself with a sledge hammer. I thought that was normal. It was a big shock to experience something more gentle. It's taken me time to adjust."

Eating Sober

What about another basic: food? Few recovering people don't experience some pretty illuminating if not downright strange realizations in this area.

A couple of examples:

- "My pattern of eating when I drank was simple," says Mark, a forty-two-year-old accountant in New York. "I'd drink gallons of water, coffee, and juice in the morning because I was so dehydrated. God, there was nothing like that awful thirst. I used to keep a liter-sized soda bottle full of water next to my bed every night. After I passed out, my thirst would usually wake me up several times, and the bottle was almost always empty by the time I finally got out of bed, still dying for water. So breakfast was liquid. Lunch was, too, only a different kind: vodka-and-grapefruit, usually, at this Irish bar I went to on the stroke of twelve noon, escaping from my office as quickly as I could. 'Lunch' could last up for one and one-half to two or three hours, depending on whether my boss was also out on a lunch date. As I got to know our clients and their degree of longwindedness, I could predict almost to the minute how long he'd be out. Anyway, I'd slog through the rest of the day, head back to my Irish bar as soon as the second hand passed five o'clock, drink my way to midnight or however long I could last, then fall into a cab and be let off at an all-night Chinese takeout place a block away from my apartment building. I'd suddenly be ravenous for the greasiest, gloppiest stuff they had. I'd get a gallon container of fried God-knows-what, drag it home, and pig out, half-conscious, until I was ready to pass out. Pig out and pass out, that about sums it up."

Mark lets out a pained laugh. "And now—I don't know. Now that I'm not drinking, it's like I've discovered food for the first time. I'm eating more than I ever did. Partly it's anxiety. Partly it's to fill up the void that booze used to fill. Party it's because, for the first time, I can actually *taste* the stuff. I can't seem to stop eating! My sponsor and friends in the program tell me not to worry. I'm doing just fine, they say, as long as I don't drink. I can put this problem 'on the shelf' for the time being. But I can't help worrying. I'm turning into a blimp. How am I gonna attract anybody? I mean, now that I'm not drunk all the time, you know, I wanna, like, eventually anyway, meet some women. Nobody would take a second look at me the way I am now. . . ."

Mark pauses for a moment, then continues, his voice a bit softer. "I am a compulsive person. That's become absolutely clear. I'll latch on to anything I can to get out of myself: food, sex, sleep, you name it. Sometimes I feel like a fake. Sure, I've given up booze, but what's the point if I keep acting out in every other way? It's hard to believe things will get better just by not drinking and by going to a meeting every day. I feel like how I am now is how I'll always be. But maybe I'll be able to 'turn this over' too, like everybody keeps telling me to do. I went to an Overeaters Anonymous meeting once, and freaked out. I mean, I identified with everybody there, but I knew it was too soon for me to get involved. I guess I've accepted that it's all I can do right now to keep from drinking every day. People in AA tell me not to get into a relationship or make any big changes in my first year, and just trust that, in time, all this stuff will get dealt with." Mark pats his considerable belly, and looks up, a half-pleading look in his eyes. "I just wish I had a little less to deal with!"

• Isabel's dilemma about food is in some ways the opposite of Mark's. She's hyperconcerned about nutrition, and a stickler about the amount (low) and quality (high) of what she eats. "It's outrageous that recovering alcoholics and drug addicts aren't told more about nutrition," she says. A sixty-five-year-old grandmother who works part time for a health clinic that specializes in nontraditional preventive healing and medical practices, Isabel holds some fierce opinions on this topic. "All right. I know that when I drank, which I did for over forty years, I couldn't have cared less about good nutrition; I didn't have a clue what it was. Then I started working at this clinic about five years ago. I think it was God readying me for the changes he wanted me to make that put me here. Not that my eating habits changed right away. But I was learning about good diet—high complex carbohydrates, lots of vegetables and fruits, very little animal protein, no added fat, sugar, or salt—and at least I began to see the wisdom of it, even in my drunken or hungover state!" Isabel's anger gathers steam.

"Now I go to meetings and I see Oreos and coffee—sugar, fat, and caffeine—and I think, heavens, it's no wonder so many people can't stay off booze and go out again. With the mood swings you go through anyway in sobriety, dosing yourself regularly with sugar and caffeine is like rubbing salt—another no-no, come to think of it!—into a wound. And the smoking! How can a recovering alcoholic call himself recovering when he's consuming nicotine, caffeine, and sugar all day? It makes me so mad to see all these people making it so needlessly difficult for themselves!"

This is a familiar and galling rage for Isabel. "The stupidity and the—the *injustice* of it! Don't these people know what they're doing?" She shakes her head in exasperation, sighs, "But what can you do?" and manages to calm down a little. "My sponsor tries to remind me that imposing my view of the world on everybody isn't going to do anybody much good, least of all myself. 'Let go and let God,' she says. 'Live and let live.' 'Don't take anyone else's inventory.' And she keeps saying that any anger, even justifiable anger, is dangerous." Isabel pauses for a moment. "That does get through to me, about the anger. Because when I let myself get into one of these rages, I do automatically think of having a drink. And then I think, how can I set myself up as this nutritional know-it-all when I'm so ready to start ruining my own health with alcohol?"

Isabel confesses to another difficulty. "It's this rage for perfection. I mean, stopping drinking meant to me that I was supposed to stop everything. For the last couple of years I'd already been eating—when I ate at all—fairly healthily. In fact, I'd put a lot of hope into good nutrition, thinking it would allow me to drink the way I wanted to. But now, here I am, a sixty-five-year-old grandmother, and I think sometimes I might be anorexic. Isn't that only fourteen-year-old girls? It's just that—well, any extra ounce makes me depressed. I'm determined to be as thin as I can be. So, sometimes, I don't eat. . . ." But Isabel keeps talking about it. "My sponsor has been through this too. I realize it's her love and care, and the love and care of my friends in AA, even if they do drink coffee and eat Oreos, that are saving my life. They all tell me I don't have to be perfect. And that I can eat when I'm hungry." Isabel pauses again. "I don't know. It's hard. 'One day at a time' . . ."

What we experience physically in sobriety poses any number of challenges, and there seem to be few easy answers. Certainly, there's a great deal more to explore in this area. And while we can't hope to say anything definitive in the space of this chapter or book, we'll be investigating numerous additional physical challenges in sobriety as we go on. But in the spirit of the Twelve Step slogan "Keep it simple," it might be appropriate to pause for a moment and simply take stock of what your physical sobriety *feels* like, without getting too complicated about it. A simple awareness of the physical changes you're experiencing, or even acknowledging that you *are* a physical being, can, on the most basic level, be healing—perhaps revelatory—even if, as in Isabel's and Mark's cases, you may not come up with any easy solutions or answers. Isabel said later that just giving vent to her rage about poor nutrition, just admitting that she feared she might be anorexic, has been healing in itself. Admitting your own awarenesses can have the same effect.

Celebration Anxiety

The first ninety days of sobriety can be an Alice-in-Wonderland explosion: Suddenly, the world may somehow appear simultaneously starkly real and fantastic, a new place with new rules.

But even if your first days and weeks of sobriety do not strike you with that kind of dramatic force, there is almost always some sort of awakening: a kind of dipping-your-toe-into-the-water, an acquaintance with some surprising new ways of living and feeling. Anxiety can alternate with feelings of well-being, boredom, rage, sadness, and hilarity (Twelve Step meetings can be very funny, even if you may not always know what everyone's laughing at).

A good deal of anxiety, however, often relates to completing that magical-sounding "ninety days." Twelve Step programs sometimes do, wittingly or not, put a good deal of pressure on completing "ninety and ninety" (ninety meetings in ninety days), the period of abstinence traditionally suggested to newcomers to see if sobriety is what they want. It's the rare recovering addict or alcoholic who doesn't feel some trepidation about facing what comes after this period; you might call it the "Now what?" syndrome. Let's take a closer look at this common anxiety, not least because it will prepare you for the future "Now what's?"—like when you complete your first six months, year, two years, and so on of sobriety. One day at a time.

"I was not what you'd call your average, willing, recovering drunk," states Hal, a thirty-three-year-old Minneapolis man. "I remember going to a couple of AA meetings when I still drank; in fact, I went drunk, although not so drunk that anyone could tell right off. In fact, they used to call on me when I raised my hand. No doubt with profound regret afterward. I'd tell them what a bunch of tight-ass schoolmarms they all were, and that what they really needed was to tie one on and get laid. I don't think I was everybody's favorite speaker.

"But . . . well, even I knew when I was through. Or at least the courts did." Hal's drinking had lost him everything: his wife ("She didn't even bother to try to get alimony—hell, for the last five years, I was the one mooching off her; she knew there wasn't a chance in hell of getting any money out of me"), his job as a salesman for a plumbing supply company ("The only plumbing I ever paid attention to was my own"), and his home. He was living on the streets for about a year before getting thrown into and out of jail and into a detox. "I was in jail because I got mad at this jerk bartender in a fleabag bar who wouldn't serve me a drink even after I offered to wash his goddamn window. I threw a rock through it instead. Cops came, and jail and detox dried me out."

Hal doesn't know why this was his "bottom"—"It's not like it was much different from two hundred other scenarios I'd gone through in the last ten years of my drinking life"—but something in detox got through to him. He didn't have much truck with the "damned God talk" he heard during the in-house AA meeting he went to, but one day a guy came in to chair the meeting, a guy who'd been in the same detox himself, had had a job Hal used to have, lost it, and got it back again. "He was like, I don't know, the 'me' I never could be. He was a success. Every time before now when I saw some guy I thought was successful, it was like he came from another planet. Couldn't relate. But this guy, I don't know. I could relate." The speaker ended up becoming Hal's sponsor and taking him to his first AA meeting out of detox.

Hal responded at first like a grumpy kid. "I didn't want to drink. I had to admit, that was amazing. But I sure as hell didn't want to do whatever the hell the 'program' wanted me to do. Not that I exactly knew what that *was.* I mean, I still can't make head or tail of the Twelve Steps. It's all Greek to me. But, I don't know, it's like I didn't want all those sober people pulling me in. I kept wondering what their angle was. What they wanted out of me. What the deal was."

The deal, Hal's sponsor told him, was simply to give it ninety days. Don't drink for ninety days, and go to a meeting every day for ninety days. The only AA slogan that Hal could make any sense of was "One day at a time." "I could figure that out," Hal

says. "That's how I used to drink. Every day, one day at a time."
As his ninety days began to go by, one by one, a week, two weeks,
a month, two months, two and a half months, Hal experienced
something strange and new. "My sponsor said it was self-esteem.
I suddenly had some. I guess he was right." But as the ninetieth
day drew near, Hal began to feel uncomfortable, really uncomfortable. Scared. Even, he admits, terrified. "How could I keep
this up? It was like somebody hoodwinked me into staying off
booze for ninety days, but now, hell, I couldn't continue this.
Not drink for the rest of my life? Who was I kidding? I couldn't
keep this up, that's what I kept telling myself, I couldn't keep
it up. . . ."

Hal says that on the morning of the ninetieth day he came
very close to picking up a drink—right after he'd picked up his
welfare check. "I felt wacko," he says. "On one hand I felt proud:
I'd done it, I'd stayed off booze for nearly three months. Never
managed to do that in my whole adult life before. On the other
hand, I felt, hey, I must be cured. If I managed to stay off booze
for three months, it must be that I'm not an alcoholic! On the
other hand—whoops, that makes three hands. Anyway, I also felt
like it was time to show everybody what a mess I really was.
Yeah, I guess that was the strongest feeling. It was like I'd been
pretending to be this good guy, this model nondrinking good guy,
for a whole ninety days. But nobody realized what a jerk I still
was. I'd show them. I'd let the whole goddamn world see who I
really was. I'd get blitzed. . . ."

All these feelings buzzed in Hal as he went to his check-
cashing place, got his hundred some-odd bucks, and rounded the
corner to a liquor store. Right next to the store was a pay phone.
In Hal's pocket was a quarter. He got an idea. "I figured I'd call up
my sponsor and let him know what a fuck-up I was. You know,
really let him have it. Goddamn chump, I thought. I'd show him
I had *him* fooled." Hal dialed his sponsor at work and delivered
the news that he was a "fuck-up" and was about to get blitzed on

his ninetieth day. His sponsor calmly told him that he'd never met an alcoholic, drinking or nondrinking, who didn't at one point or another think he was a "fuck-up," and that Hal could do whatever he wanted to, but he might want to consider going to a noon meeting two blocks away before he made any final decisions.

For some reason, Hal did so. And the meeting spoke to him in a different way than a meeting ever had before. For one thing, the secretary asked if anyone was celebrating ninety days or a "birthday" of a year or more. Hal found himself raising his hand and confessing that this was his ninetieth day. Much applause. Hal felt himself going red. And feeling pleased. Later, during the sharing, people talked about how uncomfortable they always were when they faced an upcoming "birthday." "I feel like an impostor." "Don't know if I can keep it up." "Always hated all this positive attention—felt like there were too many expectations on me." "Can't accept hearing anything good about myself." In other words, Hal's soul was being bared by a young schoolteacher, a kid in graduate school, a smartly dressed career woman, and a middle-aged mailman.

"I wasn't the only one who felt the way I did—scared of doing something good for myself," Hal says. "Amazing stuff. I could— more to the point, I *wanted* to—see what day ninety-one might be like, without picking up."

I've given you Hal's story because so many recovering people have difficulty with "birthdays" or "anniversaries," whether of ninety days, one year, five years, or twenty years. "I'm so used to thinking bad stuff about me," Hal says, "that the hardest thing I face in sobriety is accepting that there might be something good in me." Even people who rejoice in reaching milestones like ninety days—and they constitute a large group too—generally understand the struggle Hal talks about. The struggle is complicated. Even when you *think* you're celebrating, sometimes old negative feelings can be gnawing away underneath. For example, Lois's experience on reaching ninety days:

"Celebration is called for as you reach a birthday or anniversary," Lois says. "My lover, Rosa, got sober a year before I did, and she was as happy as I was when I reached my ninety days. It seemed like a miracle. We'd spent so much time in bars; that's where we met, after all. And all our women friends still drank. It was so much part of the lesbian scene, at least for the people we knew. So when she took me out to dinner and had a special cake ordered, it was great. But—I don't know—I got so manic. I had this horrendous headache all through dinner. I felt such incredible—*pressure*, I guess. And I realized there had never been another so-called celebration in my life, past birthdays, graduations, getting this or that award, when I hadn't also felt this same kind of pressure. It was like I couldn't accept I was doing it for myself—that I was doing it for *me*. It all felt like some performance I was doing for someone else's benefit. . . ."

Lois says that Rosa, her friends in AA, and her sponsor all have been "incredibly supportive, telling me it's okay to feel whatever I feel, including terrible," even when circumstances (like reaching her ninety days) seem to make negative feelings inappropriate. "I know I'm struggling with old childhood issues. I had to *behave* all the time; it was like everything I did, I did for my mother, never for me. So it's hard to accept that sobriety is something I'm doing for myself. . . . But then I think, who else could I be doing it for? It only *works* when I realize I'm doing it for me."

Yet another perspective about birthdays and anniversaries in sobriety, especially the special ninety-day one, comes from Jacob, a fifty-year-old professor at a small New England college. "The most reassuring thing I've ever heard in AA," Jacob says, "is that the person who's been sober the longest is the person who got up earliest. It takes the pressure off anniversaries for me to realize that. Sobriety only exists in the moment, right now. That's all I need to remember. Sure, it's nice to realize you've made ninety days. It's a great feeling. But life has a way of continuing. And you find yourself living ninety-one days. And ninety-two. And, if you're lucky, a hundred. And more.... Assumptions break down; a whole new way of looking at life and time starts to grow. Nothing is more healing to me than this realization: It's what's going on right *now* that counts."

It won't surprise you to hear that the anxiety, joy, fear, anger, boredom, awakening, and confusion we've just seen—the power of which can be so overwhelming in the first ninety days—don't disappear after three months. As your vision of the world slowly changes, as the prism of your perspective shifts, these feelings may start to change; they may spill into each other, intensify, fade, reemerge differently. But, on the evidence of hundreds of recovering people, they won't go away.

How do you deal with all this now that you've decided not to erase everything with a drug or a drink? If you go to Twelve Step meetings, you'll often hear one of two simple answers: "Work the Steps" or "Work your program." What does this mean exactly? How do you make sense of the "program" in your first days of sobriety?

As with everything else, recovering alcoholics' and addicts' experiences with and reactions to Twelve Step programs vary. But the question about the "program" and doing the "Steps" is an urgent one for nearly everybody who starts going to Twelve Step meetings. Let's tackle it head on.

two

Climbing the Steps

Walking into an AA or NA meeting for the first time can be intimidating. To some newly recovering people it just seems like one more club to which they feel they have little hope of learning the password. The Twelve Steps, the Twelve Traditions, neatly lettered signs listing something called "the Promises" and any number of slogans on the wall—and the jargon! What is everybody talking about? All this stuff about "turning it over," "Twelve Stepping," "the hole in the doughnut," "the Seventh Step prayer," "layers of the onion," . . . (What the hell is *on* "page 449 of the Big Book," anyway? Never mind that—what is the Big Book?) The format of the meetings can be baffling. Why does nobody "cross talk"? Why do people applaud?

Few alcoholics and addicts I've met are comfortable with the idea of joining a group. Many of us just assume we don't fit in *anywhere*, an assumption that can make us highly resistant to feeling like one of the gang at a Twelve Step meeting. Whatever we hear that we don't understand often just makes us feel more separate, and can reinforce what we're already convinced is our permanent outsider status.

Not that this is everyone's response to their first Twelve Step meeting. Sometimes the only thing you feel (blessedly) is relief, the relief of finding something—anything—that promises to offer some respite from the addictive pressures and pains you can't bear anymore. You may be willing to sit for hours waiting for the "troops" to come marching in. It almost doesn't matter what anybody is talking about. The sheer fact that they're *there* may be enough.

You've undoubtedly heard both of these polar responses to Twelve Step meetings—from bewildered wariness to an immediate embrace—and much of what comes in between. And you probably have a fair idea where you are in that spectrum. You may in fact find yourself in more than one part of it, depending on how you happen to be feeling that particular day—perhaps leaning a bit more toward "embrace" at one moment, toward "wariness" the next.

But is there a "right" place to be on the spectrum? Are there any hard-and-fast shoulds and shouldn'ts in Twelve Step programs? Is there any "correct" way, for example, to do the Twelve Steps? (Do you have to do the Steps at all?) Or is it all "take what you want and leave the rest"?

Recovering people have a wide range of responses to the challenges set by Twelve Step principles. Perhaps nowhere is our diversity as recovering alcoholics and drug addicts more evident than in how we individually accommodate ourselves to "the program." From my observations (and the memory of my own painful experience), I've seen people in their first year of recovery get pretty panicky about it. The instinct to berate ourselves for our imperfections and inadequacies can propel us unmercifully. We may strive to be the Most Efficient Recovering Person in History, or we may run to the other extreme, hanging on to the "Let go" part of "Let go and let God," feeling completely unmoored and isolated, and often dangerously close to resuming our old self-destructive behavior.

Our aim is to show you a number of varying approaches to "the program." We're not offering a guide to doing the Steps; plenty of other literature exists to do that. We're more interested in the range of *attitudes* first-year recoverers have brought to dealing with Twelve Step program issues, one or more of which might ring true for you or, perhaps, shed some light on a path you haven't tried yet and might want to.

Let's start with one of the first, most pressing dilemmas recovering people in Twelve Step programs seem to face: the prospect of getting a sponsor. Or rather, first, deciding whether or not to get a sponsor, then, how to choose one if you decide you want one, and how to deal with the sponsor once you've got him or her. (Or them! As you may already know, you can have more than one.)

The Search for a Good Heart: Joys and Terrors of Having a Sponsor

"The only requirement for membership in Alcoholics Anonymous is"—Andrew says his sponsor, Tim, would often add a "damn it!" for emphasis, so exhausted was Tim from repeating this so often—"*the desire to stop drinking.*" Andrew laughs a little guiltily. "I *was* pretty impossible," he says. "Not that I'm especially 'possible' now. But I'm a little better." What was Andrew doing that so exhausted and exasperated Tim? "Tim kept trying to remind me that the desire to stop drinking was the only rule AA sets for membership, that all the other stuff is *suggestion*, because I was trying to rampage through sobriety like Carrie Nation." Andrew looks sheepish. "I'd rail at him: What about all the stuff I keep hearing I'm supposed to do? Won't I go back to drinking if I don't do it? Shouldn't I be doing more service, making coffee, chairing meetings, attending AA conferences, getting sponsees of my own, speaking at prisons and hospital detoxes, Twelve Stepping bums on the street, working on my Fourth Step? I keep hearing if I don't work my program as hard as I can, I'll go back out there! If I don't 'give it away,' I can't keep it. Isn't that right? Huh? *Isn't that right?*"

Andrew's eyes would now narrow, he says, as he peered into

his sponsor's tired eyes. "What kind of sponsor are you, anyway? Shouldn't you be cracking the whip a little?" Andrew says he'd heard from so many people in the rooms that they got "tough love" from their sponsors. Sponsors who cracked whips were the best, surely. But Tim didn't seem willing to do that.

In his first three months of AA, Andrew was already on his fourth sponsor, so he felt he knew something about the subject. "My first sponsor was Italian, this wonderfully handsome man, movie star material, all sleek dark hair and European savoir faire. I thought, boy, if I could be like him, I'd be perfect. I'd met him at the first gay AA meeting I went to. He had about a year and a half sobriety; I had about a week. I was so vulnerable. But so, I guess, was he. It was a disaster." It was indeed. Andrew's first sponsor ended up going back "out." Andrew was afraid it was the result of the stormy breakup they'd had when Andrew announced that he didn't think he ought to have a sponsor who was also his lover, and he felt responsible. He felt so guilty, in fact, it almost sent *him* back to booze and drugs too.

But somehow he managed to hang on long enough to find another sponsor, a maternal woman in her fifties who was, he says, "so sweet and so quiet and so terrified of saying anything she felt I didn't want to hear that we never had real conversations. She's still a great friend—but not who I needed as a sponsor." His next sponsor was a heterosexual, conservative businessman who was out of town more than in town; unfortunately, even when he was in town Andrew had less than fully satisfying exchanges with him. "The guy just didn't have much"—Andrew struggles for the right word—"*feel* for the struggles of a recovering gay man. He'd start to look a little sick—he'd actually get white all of a sudden—when I started to tell him about all the druggy sexual messes I used to get myself into. He just couldn't relate. All he could do was give me chapters to read in the Big Book."

Andrew was now on a program warpath. He was damned if this new sponsor, Tim, wasn't going to work. He liked Tim; he seemed approachable, quiet, hip enough to take Andrew's stories of excess, even if he wasn't gay. (Andrew says he never wants to risk repeating the "Italian experience.") But all Tim kept telling him was, "Relax."

Andrew was not pleased. Or at least not until he allowed himself to calm down a little and listen a little more closely to what his sponsor meant by "relax." Tim apparently said something like this: "Look, you're in your first year. Take all the time you need to get used to the very first Step. See if you even agree with it! *Are* you powerless over alcohol and drugs? Has your experience really taught you that? Meditate on it a little. Think. Get a feeling for what 'unmanageability' is all about. Beyond getting evicted from your apartment or losing your job or getting two teeth knocked out by a bouncer at that last after-hours club you went to. Think about what unmanageability feels like *inside*. The despair, the black void of it. The hunger for something that will fill you up. Think of what it meant to you—what it means to you, now, really, to surrender."

Andrew smiles. "I began to realize I'd finally found the right sponsor," he continues. "It's not that Tim doesn't want me to 'work my program.' It's just that he wants to make sure whatever I'm going through has meaning. That I give myself the chance to see what I'm doing before I jump in and do it. That's pretty incredible. Nobody has invited me to slow down like this before. I'm actually getting a glimmer of what it might be like to feel serenity."

Andrew says that the fact that Tim isn't gay doesn't matter the way it seemed to matter with his businessman sponsor. "Tim says that all he cares about is that I feel comfortable telling the truth, no matter what the truth is. He says he doesn't have to understand every reference; it's all right that some of the particulars of my 'war stories' are different from his. He says something I think is wonderful: '*Truth will resonate in a good heart.*' The only thing he doesn't want to hear from me is a lie. Although, even if I tell him lies, I have the feeling he won't judge me." Andrew shakes his head, lets out a low sigh. "Boy," he says quietly, "imagine that. Someone who won't judge me."

If you've been to Twelve Step meetings of any kind, you've heard how important it can be to choose a sponsor and work closely with him or her. And if you're like so many of the rest of us, you've had some fears and confusion about what the sponsorship relationship is supposed to be all about. Is it getting a surrogate parent or teacher? Is it simply a casual friend you bump into now and then and share a few thoughts with? Should the person you choose be someone who's like you, or someone who's different? Older or younger? How much sobriety should she or he have?

Again, it's not the place of this book to answer these questions. So much other literature exists to guide you here. In fact, Alcoholics Anonymous puts out a leaflet on what sponsorship is meant to be, making it clear that there's a great deal of leeway in this area. It says, in fact, that there is no "best way" of sponsoring a newcomer. In other words, it's pretty much wide open.

The literature of Alcoholics Anonymous does strongly suggest that you get a sponsor, but it leaves the details to be worked out by the prospective sponsor and sponsee. Andrew makes clear what his own particular lesson has been from this relationship: "Tim lets me know that I've got to learn about and then follow my own heart. If I do too many things by rote, I'll start to feel separate from what I'm doing; it won't have any real meaning or value to me. And I'll end up screwing up again. Going back to booze and drugs."

This isn't to say that some people don't benefit from a much more structured approach than Tim is taking with Andrew. Joyce, who by her own admission has had "more slips than Macy's lingerie department," learned the hard way that she needs to follow to the letter every concrete suggestion she can get about staying sober. "In my last rehab, they had us work through all the Steps in a month. I'd been to enough AA and NA meetings in the past to know it was reasonable to question this. How could I possibly do all these Steps in a month? Why, I knew college professors who'd been sober for years and still hadn't gotten to the Fourth Step! God, was I haughty. I said it was a matter of preference, and how dare they coerce me! I was just too emotionally burdened and sensitive to do a fearless moral inventory just then, thank you very much." Her rehab counselor's ears were deaf to all that. "I still had to do it. And now," Joyce says, "I'm glad I did. It doesn't matter that I didn't do all the Steps perfectly. It matters that I now have some personal hands-on experience of what they *are*." Now that Joyce is out of rehab, she's found that she needs a strong sponsor. In fact, she has two sponsors: "A woman who I feel I can talk to about my children, and an older man who's been in the program for twenty years and gives me real old-fashioned AA. He can quote chapter and verse from the Big Book. Anything I complain about, he tells me which step to work on. There's not a whole lot of margin for me in sobriety, at least not right now. I'll die if I go out there again. So, as the Big Book says, I'm 'willing to go to any length' to stay sober. And if that means standing on my head while reciting the Twelve Steps backwards, get me a cushion to put my head on right now, and here I go. . . ."

Andrew would not be happy with the by-the-book sponsor Joyce has; Joyce might be back out there drinking if she had Tim as a sponsor. They've each found people who fit them. Not everyone needs a sponsor to be a friend; in fact, as was made clear in Andrew's "Italian experience," too much intimacy between sponsor and sponsee can be disastrous. But neither does it seem to be a good idea to use your sponsor as a therapist. Sponsors are *people*—people who used to get drunk or high and are grappling with the same stuff in sobriety that you are. At the most basic level, the sponsor and sponsee relationship is simply that of one recovering drunk or addict helping another to stay sober.

What about people who don't get a sponsor, and don't seem to want or need one? From my cross-country observations of people in their first year of sobriety, it's clear to me that even those people who don't have a formal sponsor relationship generally have friendships that perform the same function; that is, friendships with sober people they can rely on to talk about what's bothering them. It's equally been my observation that people who *don't* have these friendships—whether they apply the label of "sponsorship" to them or not—end up feeling isolated and miserable.

We started this part of the book by saying how alone and isolated many of us automatically felt when we first approached Twelve Step meetings—how, as a whole, we're not generally crazy about joining a group. This feeling of isolation clearly is a killer to recovering alcoholics and addicts. As I'm sure you've seen in your own life, we truly feel sober only when we feel connected. Despair, for most of us, comes from feeling the opposite: that we're lone asteroids somewhere out in space. But when we acknowledge and celebrate how much we have to share with one another, and how much solace and health there is to be found in that sharing, we seem to get better. This doesn't mean that there's anything wrong with having a "lone" nature. Many of us delight in being alone. But we do seem to need to remind ourselves that we're not alone in the universe, and to turn toward one another for help, comfort, and guidance when we need it. I haven't met a recovering person yet who didn't need that help, comfort, and guidance on a very regular basis—a *daily* basis, in most cases. Hence, again, the wisdom of "Don't drink; go to meetings." The "go to meetings" half at least partially means, "Go to people who will understand what you're going through," people you find you can let into your life. Whether the friendships we grow to depend on are "sponsorship relationships" or not, they do seem to end up saving our sanity.

The sponsor/sponsee relationship can also drop-kick you into some sense of what it's like to have a close, one-on-one relationship at a time when, commonly, it's the last thing you feel capable of. Arlene, a glamorous redhead who at forty-two has been everything from an international airline stewardess to a go-go girl in Seattle to a drug smuggler, and who's managed to amass four months of sobriety in NA, says, "I was relationshipped-out by the time I was ready to get clean. I'd gotten to the point where there were only three reasons I could ever imagine two people having anything to do with each other: sex, money, or drugs. The idea of any kind of selfless friendship was totally foreign to me. Or at least it was until I met my sponsor, Suzanne. She is just always *there* for me. Nobody, not anyone in my family, nobody I ever slept with or got married to, nobody in my *life*, has ever offered me that before. Just to be there for me." Arlene suddenly laughs. "I don't have the social skills for this stuff! I mean, I don't know what you *say* to someone who just wants to be your friend. I feel that way in NA sometimes too. I often get to meetings late and leave early because I'm petrified to actually talk to anybody before or after the meeting. Thank God meetings don't require anything of me but to sit. I just don't feel I can do much else right now. Except talk to Suzanne. Who just keeps on—well, *being* there. Sometimes I wonder what she gets out of it. In fact, I ask her that. 'Suzanne, honey, what's in this for you?' She says 'a lot.' She says putting up with me is helping her as much as it does me. God knows how. But—hey, I'll keep things just the way they are. Suzanne tells me I'll understand more about all this someday. . . ."

Invitation to the Dance:
The Steps and First-Year Sobriety

Many recovering addicts and alcoholics seem to delight in heresy, or at least in bucking the system. So many of us have balked at orthodoxy for so long that we get very uncomfortable when there's any hint of authority taking over and telling us what to do. Remember Pablo? "Don'-fuckin'-tell-*me*-what-to-do-man!" was his motto. With perhaps different words, many of the rest of us similarly bristle at the least sign of "You must do this" from anyone—whether spouse, lover, friend. boss, family, or even people in AA.

But this very mistrust of authority may work in our favor. By making sure that no one voice is any louder or more influential than any other, we stay true to the heart of how and why the Twelve Step approach works. Andrew's sponsor, Tim, was reminding Andrew of something very crucial when he repeated Alcoholics Anonymous's sole requirement for membership: a desire to stop drinking. Andrew quotes Tim further on the subject: "That means you don't have to say you're an alcoholic to belong. You don't have to do the Steps. You don't have to get a sponsor. You don't have to pay any dues or sign any documents. You don't have to do *anything*—not even stop drinking! All AA says is you have to *want* to stop drinking. And even that's not especially restrictive. Nobody's waiting at the door to determine whether or not you've got a genuine desire to stop drinking. All of that's up to you."

Realizing how great the latitude is in Twelve Step programs can be a shock, however, especially to newcomers who haven't had any experience with anything so laissez-faire or open-ended. So many of us steel ourselves to be told what to do, because that's what our experience of the world has always been: people telling us (often angrily) what to do. Because so many of us got into such horrendous trouble when we were "out there," it's what we've come to expect from nearly any relationship or group situation we get into. And now, all that *this* group requires of us is a desire to stop drinking or drugging. It can be unnerving, to say the least.

But the permissiveness of Twelve Step programs ends up benefiting so many of us. Making the *desire* to stop drinking or drugging the only qualification for membership—and even then a qualification you decide for yourself whether you've got—can prove to be the source of some our deepest healing. This same permissiveness is built into every "Step" and "technique" you'll hear about in Twelve Step programs. Everything is offered as *suggestion*. The program thus becomes an open invitation: We're encouraged to accommodate ourselves to these suggested Steps and traditions in whatever ways we find most comfortable and effective. Not that there's any lack of guidance. In fact, as you've already discovered if you've begun to read the copious literature Twelve Step programs make available, there's barely a square inch of recovery that AA or NA or any of the other Twelve Step programs haven't made a very conscientious attempt to prepare you for. But nobody is *requiring* us to do any of it. Nobody will throw us out if we do something "wrong." There's nobody, anyway, who *could* make such a requirement: No one person or small decision-making group rules Alcoholics Anonymous or any other Twelve Step program. The decisions that do periodically need to be made to keep Twelve Step organizations afloat are always the product of wide consensus. There's no one behind the scenes taking over and running things.

Freedom can be scary. An animal that's spent all of its life in a cage sometimes won't come out when the door is finally opened. Like that animal, we may get so used to being and feeling imprisoned that we can't imagine life any other way.

Garrett, a junior high math teacher in one of Brooklyn's more dangerous schools, is one person who admits to this fear of freedom. "All around me is chaos," he says. "Kids hide weapons; teachers get knifed; we've now got armed guards in the halls. It's a miracle when I can actually get my kids quieted down enough to teach them anything. Of course, smoking pot and drinking, which is what I was convinced I needed to medicate myself, hardly helped my world to get more orderly. I *thought* for a long time that's what pot and wine could do, calm me down and straighten me out" (Garrett closes his eyes for a moment and shakes his head at the absurdity of that), "but it just slowly ate away at any inner security, any chance at serenity I might ever have had. Soon the inner me was as chaotic as the outer me."

Garrett got so stoned and drunk one August night that he found himself wandering around Brooklyn's Prospect Park after dark. It was a hot night, and ex-hippie that he was, he didn't see any reason not to take his clothes off and cool down in one of the park's ponds. He stripped, splashed around for a few minutes, and went back to where he thought he'd left his clothes. No clothes. "That also meant no wallet," he says. "It also meant that here I was buck naked in the middle of the night in one of the city's—shall we say—less than desirable neighborhoods. In fact, at that very moment I could just make out a gang of kids roving toward me—right on cue. They must have seen me in the distance, but it was so dark they couldn't have seen I was naked. I heard a kid shout, 'Get him!' and the whole group ran at me like a pack of dogs. It was like some goddamn nightmare. But when they saw me naked, blathering about—I was so drunk and stoned, I couldn't get a coherent word out—they obviously felt I wasn't worth the trouble. 'He ain't got no pockets in his ass, man,' one of them said. 'Stay *away* from the fucker—he too crazy!'" Garrett says he now thinks that moment gave him the first clear clue that he had a Higher Power looking after him. "If I'd been clothed, with a wallet, I'd've been dead meat."

Garrett got out of the park by flagging down two cops in a police car who dumped him in the back seat, covered him with a raincoat, and eventually dropped him off at a detox. The Prospect Park experience was Garret's "bottom." He was ready, he says, to recover. "*Damn*, was I ready. When I got out of detox I started all but living for this terrific Narcotics Anonymous meeting. It was great because it had a lot of people who'd also mostly done pot. I've been convinced grass smokers are a little—I don't know—*strange.* In a different way from, like, coke-heads or even your average drunk. Anyway, I liked being around guys I knew could understand what I'd been through."

He was eager to get going on the Steps. "The First Step was a snap," he says. "All I had to do was remember that night in the park to remind me of powerlessness and unmanageability. And, hey, my life had been spared, so the Second Step, the idea that some Higher Power was knocking around somewhere looking after me, offering the chance at sanity, wasn't too hard to swallow, either. And I'd fallen hook-line-and-sinker for the Third Step. Turn my life over? With pleasure." Garrett felt a hunger for "getting on with it": doing the Steps as quickly as he could, so he could get—get what?

"The *prize,*" Garrett says. "I was convinced there was one. Some magical present I'd get after I'd bombed through all the Steps. Some—I don't know—moment of revelation, like finally getting a perfect solution to a complicated math problem. Unfortunately I hadn't counted on what happened to me when I bombed into the Fourth and Fifth Steps. . . ." As you probably know by now, the Fourth Step is the one where you're encouraged to make "a searching and fearless moral inventory" of yourself; the Fifth Step is where you admit "to God," yourself, "and to another human being the exact nature" of your wrongs. Garrett says he was buzzing along happily, getting a pad and pen out, writing down lists of resentments and fears just as the Big Book suggested, and then, "Suddenly I was horrified. I started really *looking* at the wreckage of my life. It was endless. This Fourth Step would have to go on forever! The most depressing part is, I'd done a lot of stuff even in sobriety that was pretty terrible. Maybe not as far out as the sexual escapades, stealing, and car crashes I'd gotten into stoned, years before. But I still wasn't behaving like I was sober. I was painting the portrait of a *monster.* It was horrible—*I* was horrible. I'd had this really nice guy for a sponsor, real easygoing. We talked a lot about baseball and stuff.

How could I tell him all *this?* How could I tell him about cheating on my girlfriend with her best friend—*after* I'd gotten sober? That I'd once come on to one of my fourteen-year-old students? How could I tell him about when I got drunk one night and threw a beer into my eighty-year-old grandmother's face because I was convinced she hated how long my hair was? I looked through my past and saw nothing but shame and disaster. I was literally nauseated by my life. I couldn't come up with one memory that wasn't an indictment of me. Then I felt panicky. There was no way I could tell anyone all of this! Did this mean I was still a conniving fraud? Well, tough shit. If I was a fraud, that's just who I was. How had I ever convinced myself I could change? I wasn't going to let anyone know the extent of how evil I really was, and always would be. I'd just have to go on doing what I used to do when I smoked dope and drank. Cover up. Not let anyone inside. Keep up a facade, keep talking about ball games with my sponsor. But then I thought, shit, if life was still going to be a cover-up, I might as well get high and at least get *some* enjoyment out of it. . . ."

Garrett had already scheduled an appointment with his sponsor to do his Fifth Step; he'd been so confident he could speed right through his Fourth Step before he'd even started it that, in his naiveté, he'd seen no reason not to just go ahead and schedule a Fifth Step confession. But now, with his litany of horrors, he couldn't go through with it. He wasn't even sure he could go on living—that was how bad he felt. He called up his sponsor and canceled.

"My sponsor asked me what happened," Garrett says. "Why did I sound so depressed? I told him not to worry about it. I was probably coming down with something, I said. We could do this some other time, okay? All I wanted to do was get off the phone. . . ." Garrett's sponsor suggested they meet anyway, just to talk, but Garrett wasn't receptive. "What's the point?" he says he replied. "To go over last night's ball game? Tough luck, man, there weren't any games last night. And I can't think of anything else to talk about." Garrett's sponsor said *he* could, and that he'd be over in twenty minutes.

"My sponsor had correctly guessed it was the Fourth Step that was screwing me up. The first thing he told me when he walked into my house was the following story. 'I don't think I ever mentioned this lady I knew once who had twenty-five years' sobriety,' he began. 'She said that after her nineteenth year she thought it might be time to do the Fourth Step. She took out an envelope, wrote about four things down on the back of it, and slapped it down on the table. 'Aha!' she said. 'My problem is I hate my mother!' "

Garrett says he must have looked dumbfounded, because that's how he felt. Then, out of nowhere, he erupted with a guffaw. "You can do the Fourth Step like that?" Garrett's sponsor said you could do the Fourth Step any way it worked. But one way it doesn't work is when it becomes a weapon to use against yourself. "And that's what you've been doing, isn't it?" Garrett said, yeah, he guessed it was.

What Garrett's sponsor was trying to reveal is something most people I've met in their first year of recovery secretly yearn to hear, but don't seem to be able to allow themselves to believe. *The Twelve Steps are there to help.* They're not there to berate or chastise. They're not there to give you a reason to beat yourself up. But they're also not there—in fact, they're not able—to give you a quick-fix cure.

Garrett was "bombing through" the Twelve Steps with the unspoken idea that if he could only "get it all done," he'd be rid of every problem in his life. It would all "go away." What he now realizes is that he was trying to get out of the Twelve Steps the same thing he'd tried to get out of drugs and wine: a quick-fix escape. Something to "take it all away." Something that would allow him to get *out* of life, not deal with it. The program was something you "got over with" as quickly as you could so you'd be "cured." "Sure," he says, "I'd heard all along the addiction was a disease, and that the best you could hope for was a daily reprieve. That the only sobriety you ever had was the sobriety you have this very moment. And that there was no such thing as a recovered addict, only a recovering one. But none of that really registered. I was still convinced somehow that there was a way out. That I could escape myself, just like I'd tried to do before with drugs and alcohol, only this time without screwing myself up."

Garrett says he's now grateful that he was brought up short by the Fourth Step and brought to realize that the point of it wasn't either to allow him to "escape" *or* to make him rub his face in the wreckage of his past life. The point was to gain *clarity* about himself. "I guess I'd always thought of the Steps like a homework assignment I might have given my own students. Something external to me. A collection of rules you had to follow if you wanted to get the 'right answer.' Now I know it's not that simple. The 'answer' is something that goes *on*. It isn't like hitting TILT in a pinball machine and getting a prize. It's like it's a series of 'answers'—answers that keep opening up on to new questions and answers in a process that goes on and on. My sponsor says the Steps aren't something you ever stop doing. They're tools you can use over and over, till the day you die."

Garrett's revelation about the Steps has made him reconsider where he is in them. "My sponsor allowed me to see that I hadn't quite done even the First Step as profitably as I might want to. If I was that scared about telling anyone about my past, if I somehow still believed it was all my fault and not at all the product of my disease, I hadn't really accepted my powerlessness, had I? And there was more stuff I wanted to think about regarding the Second and Third Steps too. Sanity and Higher Power—was I so sure I knew what any of that meant to me? I know you can't do any of this perfectly, but it's like—I don't know—I now realize I was depriving myself of some pleasure and discovery. I could spend months, even years, on one Step at a time. I didn't have to get them all done by next Tuesday. Now I realize I don't want to."

An Organic Process

I've taken pains to emphasize the enormous latitude inherent in Twelve Step programs because it's so clear to me that this is a message that urgently needs to be heard. I've seen so many recovering people in their first year get eaten up with anxiety about the possibility that they're not working the Steps quickly or effectively enough. But remember Joyce's experience too. Some people benefit enormously from getting a quick overview of the Steps: "doing" them in fairly rapid succession, generally with some pretty firm guidance from other recovering people who have followed the Step route themselves. Again, there's no one "right" or "wrong" way to do any of this. A very structured approach, with black-and-white do's and don'ts, simply works for some people and doesn't for others.

There are even people who don't formally "do" the Steps at all. One friend of mine somewhat grumpily insists that he's never written down a Fourth Step or an Eighth Step list and doesn't plan to. He's leading a productive, satisfying life and has nearly ten years in sobriety. Is he "exempt" from the Steps? Actually, when you get past his grumpiness and hear a few details about how he lives his life, you find out he's been doing the Steps quite conscientiously. He's become very clear about the consequences of his actions in his past drunken life and his present sober one. He's talked about all this with people he's close to in AA, and he listens receptively to other people's experience, strength, and hope so that he can learn from it. He's gone to great pains to patch up messes he's caused and sometimes still causes now, sober. He feels a genuine humility about his gift of sobriety, and he's become a wonderful power of example of what a "successful" sober life can be all about. He's helped a lot of other people get and stay sober. Heretic that he'd like you to believe he is, he just doesn't want to *call* what he's doing "Steps." I noted before that people who don't have a formal sponsor relationship often have other friendships that perform the same function. Similarly, people who remain sober and have happy, productive lives usually are doing some pretty complete version of the Steps whether they think they are or not, even if they may not want to call what they're doing "Steps."

What, after all, are the Steps really about? Dorothy, who's on the verge of completing her first year of sobriety, has made a particularly conscientious attempt to find out. She hasn't, she says, "actually completed any but the First Step. My sponsor encourages me to take whatever time I need to work the Steps," she explains. "There's just so much to think about and absorb about the Second and Third Steps, especially accepting that I've even *got* a Higher Power, what 'sanity' means, all of that." But her "slow approach" doesn't, she says, keep her "from making what I sometimes think of as 'raids' into the rest of the Steps. In fact, I go to a lot of Step meetings, read the literature on the Steps, and it's amazing—I feel like I'm already doing at least bits and pieces of all of them!"

Some version of the Twelve Steps seems to get done by just about any recovering person who "doesn't drink and goes to meetings." It seems we end up *wanting* to recover more the more recovery we get; it's as if we know intuitively that we need to follow the pattern set out by the Twelve Steps in order to deepen and improve our sober lives. One of the clearest observations I've made about people as they "work the Steps" is that the Steps, over time, make more and more visceral sense. You may even feel like saying "I already knew that!" as you progress from Step to Step, or you may feel that you've already done much of what you're being asked to do!

It's a particularly welcome fact that there's no timetable

involved. Nobody's clocking you or monitoring your "progress" in any kind of judgmental way. The main motivation for all of us in "working the Steps," however we decide to do it, seems to be an ongoing desire to keep getting better—for ourselves, not to impress anybody else. We do it because we want to participate more fully in life, to live as consciously, freely, and joyfully as we can. It's arguable that the Steps outline an organic process that sobriety, in a sense, *wants to create for itself*—that the Steps have codified something you're on the road to doing anyway, just as a product of not drinking and drugging, and regularly going to meetings.

Luckily, however, we don't have to reinvent the wheel—or the Steps. Most of us seem to find out sooner or later that it's easier to pay attention to suggestions others have made about their own "dance" of Steps than it is to create entirely new dances for ourselves. However, if you want to create your own dance, you can. As with so much else in recovery, it's all up to you—and your Higher Power.

The God Part

A familiar criticism leveled at Twelve Step programs is that they're God-based—that they require of their members a kind of religious conversion and commitment. This may be the single most negative assumption newcomers have about joining a Twelve Step group. It also turns out, as I think you'll see, to be a misconception. Let's let one of our most skeptical members give us some perspective about it.

"I once thought AA was just another coercive attempt to get me to believe in God," says Lucille, a sixty-year-old, highly intelligent (and highly suspicious) businesswoman from Alabama. "Wasn't it just telling you to surrender to the Great Almighty? See the error of your ways and repent? Get on your knees and pray to get saved? Admit what a terrible person you were?" Lucille looks disgusted. "None of that for *me*. I had enough of that nonsense being brought up in a Southern Baptist family!"

Lucille's drinking had always been done in private. "Well," she says, "I used to go to bars, but then about five years ago I looked at myself in a bar mirror and saw this lonely middle-aged woman drinking, and that was so depressing that I took to my room and drank there instead." Her resentment about her up-bringing and the "foolishness" of God and religion was some-thing she'd always kept to herself too, at least until she woke up eleven months ago in a hospital from a nearly successful suicide attempt ("I'd reached an unbearable point of loneliness and de-spair") and crashed into the revelation that she did, after all, want to live, and wanted to turn her life around, whatever it took. "Everyone told me to go to AA, so I did. But, willing as I was, the God stuff made me nuts. . . ."

The very wording of the Twelve Steps, of course, anticipated some of Lucille's grumbling. The Third and Eleventh Steps barely mention the word "God" before they italicize or capital-ize a quick qualification: *"AS WE UNDERSTOOD HIM."* And many members of Twelve Step programs, Lucille was pleased to observe, had no truck with the "Him" part either. "Her" or "It" were often substituted. Yet none of this quite managed to dis-lodge her assumption that AA was "religious." It was an obstacle she couldn't seem to keep from stumbling over.

Lucille elaborates. "Even when I steeled myself to actually go to a meeting and heard people talk about how you didn't have to be religious—that you could be an agnostic or atheist and still benefit from the program—I didn't really believe it. I couldn't help feeling that there was something insidious going on. Like they'd be real nice and rational, but lie in wait until you were vulnerable and then spring a 'God-net' over you. Brainwash you. Turn you into one of those Moonies."

Like many people who come into AA, Lucille's only concept of "God" came from her childhood perceptions of religion. "I couldn't go to a Second or Third Step meeting, where everyone would talk about their Higher Powers, without feeling resistant and suspicious. And when I shared, all I could think of to talk about was the prejudice and cruelty I'd experienced as a little girl, all in the name of 'God.' How I'd get slapped in church if I fiddled around too much. How my mother would threaten that I was going to hell because I was such a bad girl. That was it: God was used as a threat. The only purpose I could see in religion was to shut me down and keep me in line. It was an awful way to grow up."

The litany of abuse heaped upon religion by so many people in AA is striking. Jewish, Protestant, Roman Catholic—it doesn't seem to matter which faith anybody espoused. But Lucille became fascinated with the seemingly inescapable fact that, even with all the bad experiences it seemed so many people had had with religion, they still kept coming back to AA. She travels a great deal in her work and began to make sure to go to a lot of "Beginner" meetings wherever she went, her ears particularly pricked for information about how newly recovering people were defining all this "God stuff" for themselves. After a number of months, she began to see how wide a spectrum of belief there was in AA—a spectrum broad enough even to include her.

"Meetings do differ from place to place. On the East Coast they talk about your 'anniversary' when you've got a year or more of sobriety; other places they call it a 'birthday.' Some meetings give poker chips out to celebrate three, six, and nine months of sobriety. Some meetings give real parties with cakes. Little medallions get handed out at others. Sometimes you get a lot of literature read aloud at the beginnings of meetings. At other meetings—New York, especially, maybe because they're all so impatient!—you get right into sharing. Meetings at some places can seem like down-home old-fashioned AA; at others you'll hear some strikingly subtle and wide-ranging psychological talk. I guess I was struck by all this because I could see, built into the range of how different people spoke in different meetings across the country, that there was amazing flexibility. And the 'God talk' was similarly wide-ranging.

"After meetings I jotted down some examples of Higher Power talk to think about later. 'I didn't need God then and I don't need Him now,' one young man said. 'What I need is *you* guys—everyone who goes to a Twelve Step meeting. That's all the Higher Power I want in my life.' Or, from a newly sober priest: 'I've always loved and believed in God, but I came to realize that I was using religion as another escape—accepting the dogma of the church instead of exploring what my "love" for God really meant to me. The church couldn't, by itself, get me sober, but now that I've opened the channels in AA, I'm discovering that God can. My understanding of "God" is so much richer than it used to be.' Or this, from an ex-hippie who'd been the whole 'mind-expansion' route: 'I loved doing acid because it showed me the incredible capacity my mind had, and gave me this real sense that, you know, we're all part of one unified Creation, all connected parts of a Whole. But this was always something I had to depend on drugs to reveal to me. I never had the *personal* sense—the day-to-day sense—that I could rely on this "Oneness" to get me through the ordinary stuff of life. I thought I had to be blasted out of my mind to really feel that.' Or this, from a young lady I especially identified with: 'For all I know, something like "God" may exist. But all I know is my own experience. I have to say that when I first wanted to get sober, I did have some strange intuitive sense that I was being taken care of. It's not something I like to talk about much; it's very private. But it was like the door had opened a crack and I had some sense there was, I don't know, *light* on the other side of it, light I could somehow depend on. I don't question it much. Mostly I just try to make it through the day without drinking or drugging. But the more sober I am, the more I sort of know—have a flickering sense, anyway—what people are talking about when they talk about their Higher Powers. I guess I just have to take it slow, and let all this stuff reveal itself to me in its own sweet time. . . .'"

Lucille pauses for a moment, closes her eyes with a slight frown of concentration, then opens them and continues, choosing her words carefully. "If I'm honest with myself, I have to say I feel something like that last woman said she did. When I woke up in the hospital and realized I was still alive, I did have this strange sense that something was looking out for me. It was a comfort. And it's a comfort that continues the longer I keep from drinking and keep my attachment to AA. But it can't be pushed. My definition of 'God' has to remain vague right now, and may have to stay vague for a long time to come. Somehow, though, it doesn't seem to keep me from believing in the Second and Third Steps anymore. I have my own private sense of depending on this 'something' to restore me to sanity, and what it means to decide to turn my life over. It's fragile, but it's there. And it feels like I can build on it. . . ."

Not everyone who first gets sober is as tentative as Lucille about the "God stuff" in AA. Many people have a very strong sense of Higher Power and have no trouble feeling it and defining it for themselves. Some people very clearly connect this Higher Power with an already firm sense of God that they've gotten in their respective religions. Some people have even had the kind of mystical epiphany AA cofounder Bill W. talks about having taken place when he had his own revelation: a vision of a new and blinding light. But it's astonishing, again, to see the range of experience we bring to this aspect of AA. It doesn't seem to matter whether you've arbitrarily made the chair you're sitting in your Higher Power or you feel there's no question it's Allah, Buddha, or Jesus Christ. But whether the experience is blinding or subtle, clear or vague, we do seem, at least eventually, to plug into some sense that there's help to be had and depended on—help stronger than any we've been able to provide ourselves on our own.

A new experience of spirituality; the sense that it might after all be possible to live life consciously; the prospect that our lives might, with help, at last become "manageable": all of this is offered to us in Twelve Step programs, according to so many people who have brought a Twelve Step approach to their lives. But life can still be hard even when you're "working your program." Our feelings may still threaten to overwhelm us, even when we feel we're doing all the things Twelve Step suggestions, traditions, and literature tell us we're supposed to be doing.

Learning to deal with the onslaught of feelings in sobriety does seem to involve "using" the Steps and "working" our programs, but, on evidence, it also seems to require changing some old attitudes. In fact, to stay sober, it seems we need to change our definitions of what feelings are.

Let's meet a number of newly recovering addicts and alcoholics who are learning to do just this: change some attitudes and definitions in order to cope with feelings they once thought they could never face without drugs or alcohol.

three

Having Feelings

We characterized early sobriety in a number of ways early on in this book. One of them was that it's a little like dipping your toe into the water of a whole new way of living and feeling. "Yeah," said a recovering alcoholic friend who was eight months sober when he heard this description. "Then you get caught in a riptide and find yourself out in the middle of the ocean. Without a float."

What my friend was talking about is simple: feelings.

You may have heard the Twelve Step slogan "Feelings are not facts" and been completely baffled. They sure as hell *feel* real enough, don't they? What could that mean: "Feelings are not facts?" By the end of this chapter, I hope you'll have a clue what it might mean, as well as what it doesn't mean. From the evidence of my recovering friends, I can tell you right off that it doesn't mean feelings aren't important. Feelings are very important. They're markers telling you where you are. They can be clear signposts warning you of danger, alerting you that you've reached safety, clarifying your path in any number of ways. What they don't have to be is *you*. My recovering friends tell me that it's possible to *have* a feeling without becoming it. This may sound like semantics. In fact, it's a key to survival.

But that's jumping ahead. We need first to acknowledge something far more basic: simply that what we're talking about is new. It's not that you've never had a feeling before getting sober. It's just that, now that you're no longer drinking or drugging, your way of *dealing* with feelings has been pulled out from under you. No longer can you turn the tap on and off and escape fear, anxiety, or resentment with a drink or a drug, or induce a soporific "feel-good" state via the same means. Now that you're no longer manipulating, escaping, or steamrolling them through drinking and drugging, feelings are a whole new ball game.

The big problem—according to the scores of people I've talked to in their first year of sobriety—is that years of drinking and drugging don't prepare you for the strength of feelings that may start to pour in after you've *stopped* drinking and drugging. Not only do they come on like gangbusters, but they so rarely come on cue. Most recovering people seem to realize quickly that life is not a B movie. We may be elated, sorrowful, enraged, or numb at what seem to be terribly inappropriate times, laughing when we "should" be sad, crying when we "ought" to be happy. And the speed of mood swings can be dizzying. At one moment you might be in a state of terrible anxiety, gripped by the most compelling and intense "high drama," and the next feel like a zombie. Resentment, fear, and, especially (and most frighteningly), rage: These seem to be the broadest and most pervasive primary feelings that recovering people experience in their first year, and often for a good long time afterward. "Facts" or not, they can knock you for a loop.

Rage is often the most surprising of these emotions. So many recovering alcoholics and drug addicts who thought themselves incapable of anger—who were always the accommodating "good Joes," the "don't worry about me" doormats you could always step on (they'd never complain), the mildest wallflowers—find themselves, in sobriety, turning into towering infernos. This can be, to say the least, disconcerting.

Where does all this rage come from? And how can you survive and recover from it?

Let's see what the experience of a few people in first-year recovery can tell us, besides the fact that you're not alone if you often find yourself in what seems to be in an inexplicable, unwarrantable, but seemingly inescapable rage.

Now That I'm Sober, Why Am I So Mad?

"It was horrifying," Marcia said. "And, now that I've got some distance from it, I guess it's almost funny. The *absurdity* of it! Not that anybody was laughing at the time." Marcia was talking about an incident that had taken place the previous week with her boss. An incident fueled by feelings—including a rage—that seemed to spring out of nowhere and blast her sky-high. She's still not sure where she's landed.

But first, a little background.

Marcia, forty-three and a mother of two little boys, was widowed five years ago when her "hard-drinking" businessman husband fell over from a sudden heart attack. With what Marcia called "a typical alcoholic attitude," he had never believed he'd die and thus had minimal insurance and virtually no savings when he did die. Marcia was, she says, drinking "fairly heavily" up till then; her drinking only increased afterward. In very little time she lost her house, had to go on welfare, lived in a tiny three-room apartment with her two boys, and begged, borrowed, and stole to supply herself with liquor. Somehow she kept her family alive on food stamps, with the help of an old lady next door who looked after the kids on the frequent occasions when Marcia was too "out of it" to do so herself. "Life," says Marcia succinctly, "was hell."

Marcia hit what she calls her "bottom" about seven months ago when one of her boys, just home from school, found her passed out nude on the toilet and couldn't wake her up. He ran to their elderly lady neighbor and dragged her back to help resuscitate his mother. For some reason, Marcia took that moment to come to. "This poor little old lady was standing in my messy, reeking bathroom, with me sitting naked on the toilet seat, bombed out of my mind. . . ." Marcia shivers with remembered shame. "It's like, suddenly, some part of me popped out of the rest of me, shot up above it all and *saw* for the first time the wreck of my life. Not only what was happening in that terrible, embarrassing moment, but the *whole* wreck of my life—my feelings, my hopes—what I was doing to me and my kids. . . ." It was a powerful awakening, after which Marcia knew that she wanted to stop drinking and to seek help to stay stopped.

When her sister saw she was serious about getting sober, she offered to take care of the kids while Marcia went to rehab. Marcia was ready to get sober, and, in fact, experienced a remarkably quick physical and material recovery. "I can't believe how quickly I was able to get back on my feet again," she says. "Life has simply poured back into me, in incredible abundance. And even though my friends in recovery all told me not to make any big changes in my first year—don't stop smoking yet, they said; stay on welfare, don't worry about getting a job yet; and for God's sake don't get into a relationship yet—I did all of those things anyway. Out of the blue, a terrific job as a receptionist opened up at a local small advertising firm, just a month and a half into sobriety. I'd already lost a good deal of bloat, I knew I looked better, and I just *felt* so much better, so I applied and they took me on. Then, a few weeks after, cigarettes started to disgust me. I can't explain why this hit me when it did, but suddenly I just knew I didn't want to smoke anymore. So I quit cold turkey. Three packs a day to nothing. A week of sheer horror— God, it was worse in some ways than giving up alcohol. But I got through it, and somehow managed not to throw temper tantrums at work, though my kids bore the brunt of it at home, poor babies. And then the relationship part—two months ago I met this wonderful guy in AA. He's got two years of sobriety, and at first, when he realized I only had a few months, he tried to steer clear of me. But the chemistry was so strong. . . ."

Marcia's life sped ahead at an amazing and seemingly wonderful pitch; everything, she said, seemed "too good to be true. It was like God—my Higher Power—Who or Whatever was running things—couldn't fulfill my wishes fast enough.

"Then," Marcia pauses for a moment and seems to deflate— suddenly she looks terribly weary—"it all came to a dead halt. Or rather," she explained, "I did. It's the work thing I began to tell you about. Everything was going so well, but something inside me panicked. It's like it was all *too* good. When I look back on the explosion I went through, I can see it was building up, although I wasn't aware of it then."

The "explosion" occurred on a particularly hectic Monday morning. The switchboard flashed maniacally, and Marcia attempted to answer with her usual competence and to connect calls or take messages with her normal efficiency. But the messages, she said, "were longer than they usually were, so many people were impatient, and my boss kept trying to tell me something complicated while I was trying to answer eight calls at once. . . ." Marcia says she "lost it. I mean *really* lost it. It was like I turned into someone totally foreign—some monster I had no idea was inside me. I cut off all the calls on the switchboard, stood up in front of my boss and bellowed at him that he was an insensitive ass, and who did he think he was anyway, and I had put up with about as much abuse as I was going to. I then stormed away from my desk and out of the office, slamming the door, and ran down the stairs to the street."

Marcia cringes. "My whole body was trembling. I suppose on some level it was a relief. But the emotional aftermath, which flooded in moments after I found myself walking down the street toward the town park, was so horrible. I couldn't help replaying every moment I'd just gone through, every word of invective I'd hurled at my boss—it was like I was trapped in my rage, and it was a huge roaring in my brain. . . . I sat down on a park bench and tried to keep myself from trembling. Then I began to cry. Sob, more like it. What had just happened? I had exploded so far in excess of what the situation warranted; I mean, nothing that had happened that morning really justified this rage. Rationally, I knew that. So why couldn't I control myself? It was baffling; it was like I went crazy. Like I was somebody totally, certifiably insane."

She couldn't bring herself to go back to the office yet—"this rage turned into the deepest, deepest shame; I couldn't imagine ever showing my face in that office again"—but she thought, much as she didn't want to, she'd at least try to talk to somebody. "I didn't have a sponsor; things had seemed to be going so well in my life, I felt I didn't need one! But I could at least try to talk to Mark, my lover. He did have a couple of years of sobriety. It's funny, ever since we'd become romantically involved, I hadn't really thought of him as a 'program' person. But now I needed him to be. . . ."

Marcia called Mark at his office and told him what had happened. "Mark was so sweet. His office was nearby, and he arranged to come out to the park and meet me. I'll never forget the look on his face when he got there; he was so worried, and, it turned out, so angry with himself. He said he felt like an ass. 'I ought to have seen this coming,' he said, 'I ought to have done something—made you get a sponsor, maybe. Or—' he didn't know what to say. But he finally talked about what it was like for him when he first got sober, and what it was sometimes still like, now. 'We bottle so much up,' he said. 'And you've been trying so hard to do everything right—be the best little girl in the world. Of course you were going to explode.'

"He counseled me to sit with him for a few moments while I calmed down, then to go back to the office, apologize to my boss, and try to get through the rest of the day—call him whenever I felt I might 'lose it' again. I was so terrified of going back, but I made myself do it. And when I did"—Marcia gives a rueful laugh and shakes her head—"I couldn't believe it. My poor boss was nearly shaking. He was scared of *me*. In fact, he couldn't stop apologizing! He said he knew what a terrible morning it had been, and that he didn't want to lose me, and to please just tell him when I felt overworked and he'd see what he could do. . . . Sort of took the wind out of my sails. But it didn't keep me from doing what Mark reminded me was the 'Tenth Step': promptly admitting that I'd been wrong." Marcia exhales a long, low breath at the memory. "The frightening thing, though, was my discovery that my rage could be that strong. It meant I had to take a look at myself—really try to see what was going on."

What happened to Marcia is something that happens to many, many other recovering addicts and alcoholics. A quick overview of her situation reveals so much that is common to most of us. Mark zeroed in on it neatly: "We bottle so much up." In his recognition that Marcia was trying desperately to be "the best little girl in the world," Mark was talking about a quest for perfectionism that all too often plagues the rest of us too—an inner message we all too often give ourselves that if we're not perfect, we're failures. It's an assumption that usually leads to terrible frustration and anger, as we discover (once again!) that we can't live up to our own impossible standards.

Marcia said later that her anger shocked her: "I was never an angry person. Or maybe I never gave myself a chance to be." As Marcia thought more about how she'd dealt with feelings before she stopped drinking, she began to realize that what she did in response to *any* feeling was to drink, thereby cutting the feeling off. "I realize now that my main mission in life was to make everything 'fine.' Which really meant to make myself so out of it that nothing mattered. When nothing matters, you don't feel angry. You don't feel much of anything. I thought this was a state to aspire to. Not feeling anything. Then I couldn't be hurt. Then things wouldn't threaten me."

Marcia sums up the function of drinking and drugging for

many of us: to blot out any possibility of pain or discomfort, emotional or otherwise. "Because my life in sobriety got so good so quickly," she says, "I guess I somehow thought I'd never have a bad feeling again. But what really was happening was, I was trying to cover my feelings with work, with my relationship with Mark, with making up to my kids for not having been there for them; I was looking for some new way to cover up my feelings now that I no longer had alcohol. I thought I was getting what I wanted—great job, new lover, new life—and in some ways I was. But I was still trying to escape something essential. Who *I* really was—who I really am."

Marcia has just asked a woman with a few years of sobriety to be her sponsor, now that she realizes how much she needs more one-on-one help with the process of learning that she doesn't have to scurry away from her feelings. "I'm starting to understand, at least intellectually, that my feelings have got to come out, and that I've spent most of my life, even before I started drinking, trying to hold them down. I guess it's true what my sponsor says— that my feelings won't kill me, and that there are ways to let out my anger that won't threaten my job, my sobriety, my life—but I can't quite feel it in my gut yet. Now that I've located this rage, it seems bottomless! I'm still not sure what I'm so angry at; I only know that it feels so terribly, terribly powerful. . . ."

More Roots of Rage

George, a sixty-year-old man whose forty-year drinking and drugging career has taken him in and out of jail numerous times, landed him on the Bowery for the past fifteen years, and finally given him the clear sense that he is, as the First Step says, "powerless" over drugs and alcohol, has a different history of anger than Marcia. However, he has come up with an insight about the roots of anger that Marcia finds fully applicable to her, and that many other recovering alcoholics and addicts also find applicable to themselves.

"I sure as hell got angry when I was out there," George says. "Booze, when it got inside of me, was like gasoline waiting for a match. I got into God knows how many fights, almost killed some people, nearly got killed myself, busted up stores, committed armed robbery—believe me, they didn't keep putting me in jail for nothing. But now I'm nine months sober and nobody's putting me in jail anymore, even though I still get angry. The main thing is, I'm not drunk. Which means, somehow, I stay this side of acting completely crazy. I'm not busting up stores anymore; I'm going to AA meetings instead! But I'm also starting to see that all the stuff I thought I was angry at—the fact that I'm a black man in a racist society, had no father to speak of, junkie mother, no food or money—all that was shit, no doubt about it, and I wouldn't wish it on most dogs, but it's really an excuse. It's not that people haven't done me wrong. They have. But what I'm really angry at is something in myself. I've gone back to my church now that I'm sober, and my pastor puts it this way. He says, 'George, nobody ever told you you were all right just as you were. That God loved you all the time. God didn't care that you weren't rich or educated. God accepts you just as you are. Problem is, you haven't accepted *yourself.*'"

George's sense of injustice—of having had no privileges as a poor black man in a racist society—hides a deeper sense of injustice, and a consequent rage: rage at the idea that he is somehow constitutionally unacceptable as a human being. Marcia now realizes that she felt something similar when she blew up at her boss. "It's like my rage was searching for an outlet—any outlet—to rail against the world. I am now starting to see that what I was really mad at was the feeling that I wasn't *enough* just being me, that I couldn't feel accepted or loved for who I was, that here I was bending over backward to be the perfect receptionist to my boss, perfect lover to Mark, perfect mother to my kids, perfectly healthy nondrinking, nonsmoking woman, and even this—this supreme effort of trying to do it all, be it all, somehow *wasn't enough.*" Marcia pauses and says, "What I really need to do is accept myself. Know that I'm worth something even if I'm not perfect. If only I could make this so by saying it! And if only I could escape this terrible, terrible anger. . . . Other recovering people tell me it can happen, bit by bit. This awful feeling will lift, if I just keep on doing what I'm doing now. The old chant: don't drink, and go to meetings."

The rage Marcia and George feel is huge; it can seem, as it seems to Marcia, bottomless. It's also, as Marcia points out, always looking for outlets. "It's amazing how mad I can get at Mark for chewing too loud, or my neighbors for turning on the air conditioner when I don't think it's warm enough to waste all the energy—how angry I can get at things that aren't my business or just aren't important! It's like lava looking for cracks, looking for somewhere to erupt." George says that when he goes to AA topic meetings and the topic is anger, he sometimes can't bring himself to speak. "At just the mention of the word, I start to think of everything that makes me angry and I just sit there boiling. At least at first. Sometimes, when I calm down enough to hear that other people feel a lot like I do, sometimes I get some relief. But, my Lord, anger—it's powerful stuff."

Rage has another, perhaps even more insidious, appeal. It's a hell of an effective mood changer! Which can make it irresistible to alcoholics and addicts. "My sponsor tells me that getting angry causes an adrenaline rush, and it's like a drug high." Marcia manages to laugh a little. "God, the things I won't do to get high!" George also knows this part of anger's allure. "It gives me a rush. Gets out all this damned *energy* I got buzzing around in me. I may be sixty years old, but sometimes I think the anger in me is enough to knock out Tyson, Foreman, and Holyfield all at once!" George's hands, which have turned into fists, now relax into full palms; he spreads his arms. "Anger makes me feel *large*. That's the real deal. It makes me feel important, like I'm somebody. It gives me courage, makes me feel like a big man. I gotta admit, I love it. But I also gotta admit"—George's hands return to his sides; his voice lowers—"it could kill me. Or you, if I ever got drunk again and you're in my way."

The power of rage to alter consciousness and the deep, hurtful sense of injustice that often gives rise to rage make for a potent mix. We hate it and love it. While rage can be a powerful means of discharging energy, it's also a powerful way to make a mess of our lives, even to get us to pick up a drug or drink. The task every recovering alcoholic and addict seems to face, whether at the beginning of the first week or at the end of the second decade of sobriety, is to accept feelings, including the powerful one of rage, without allowing them to become a trigger to drink, drug, or act self-destructively in other ways. This may be the hardest but most important lesson that any recovering alcoholic or addict needs to learn, at least if he or she wants to stay sober.

We can look for help in learning this lesson from the experience of others who have survived the mine field of their own feelings. "Sometimes," as one recovering person I know puts it, "I just have to hang on so I can let go." This may sound like a paradox, but it seems to hold the key to dealing soberly with feelings.

Hanging On to Let Go

There are so many paradoxes in recovery. When asked by a newcomer in Twelve Step recovery, "What do I do to stay sober?" recovering addicts and alcoholics often feel reduced to repeating, "Don't drink, and go to meetings" because it's so hard to "explain" the magic of how recovery works in any more detailed way. One of the many paradoxes that most seems to frustrate explanation is what I've just told you my friend said: Sometimes you need to hang on to let go. This paradox has much to teach us about feelings—that you can tolerate them, that they don't have to "force" you to do anything self-destructive, rash, or irrevocable.

Matt, a twenty-five-year-old recovering crack addict and alcoholic, sheds some light on what this means. "I kept hearing 'Let go, let God' when I first came into the rooms. I thought this was great. 'Easy does it' was terrific too. It meant I didn't have to *do* anything, right? Just kind of, you know, lie back and let things happen. I could get into that. In fact, I'd been into that my whole life! You know, take a snort of something and let 'er rip. . . ."

However, Matt soon realized that "letting things happen" was pretty different from what Twelve Step people meant by "Let go, let God." He realized this when he "let go" and experienced a huge craving to go back to crack—and gave into that craving. "What happened?" Matt says he asked when he ended up in detox for the second time. "I thought I was just doing what NA and AA were telling me to do!"

Matt was "pissed" at AA and NA—and also convinced that, while they might work for "lesser" addicts, they could never work for him. "First I told myself that Twelve Step programs just weren't powerful enough to deal with crack. I mean, when Bill W. and Dr. Bob started AA, there wasn't any crack around. Shit, man, I've been drunk. I used to love to get drunk. But it was nothing compared to crack. Nothing brought me that rush, not booze, not other drugs. I felt superhuman on that stuff, man. Happy forever. Until, of course, it wore off. Which it kept doing."

Matt was going to a community college in Los Angeles when he got into crack. "I wasn't one of your usual fucked-up crack addicts, not like the press makes them out to be. I didn't come from the ghetto. I'm middle class—okay, maybe you'd call it lower middle-class, but my parents were pretty normal. I grew up in a house, got my meals. My dad drank some, but at least he was there. And my mom's okay. . . ."

Matt makes it clear that a lot of people he knew, even so-called nice people, did crack; in fact, that's how he got into it. "It was people in *college* who turned me on to it, not some sleazy drug addicts from a bad neighborhood. I thought, hell, if these guys could handle it, go to school, and get good jobs, it couldn't be that bad. And a crack high wasn't only a hell of a lot better than an alcohol high, it was, for a while anyway, a lot cheaper than getting drunk. Especially given the amount it was starting to take me to get drunk."

Matt realized it was getting out of hand when he found himself in a nearly vacant supermarket parking lot robbing an old lady, holding to her neck a switchblade he'd recently picked up at a pawn shop. "I don't know, man. Something snapped. I freaked," he says. "This old lady could've been my grandmother. That's what I was thinking—this lady has the same coat my grandmother has. All I knew up to that point was I wanted to get high and I was broke. I was doing so much crack, it wasn't cheap anymore. But, Jesus, here I was about to knife somebody's grandmother for another high. It hit me then. I hated myself for what I was doing. I just dropped her bag, you know, the money and everything. And ran the hell out of the parking lot."

Matt had known of a detox at a local hospital because he'd taken his father there after a particularly bad drunk. "Dad was a member of a real strict union that said if you got drunk a certain number of times at work you had to go into a rehab or you'd get fired." Matt didn't know if they handled crack addicts. But he came in on an atypically slow night, talked to someone who understood what he was going through, and they took him in.

"The first week or so was hell. But the people there knew what I was going through. Other guys there had just gone through withdrawal. So I got over the physical stuff and I was okay. In fact, I thought I was *really* okay. I thought all this Twelve Step crap was *easy*. They made you do the Twelve Steps—all of them—before they'd let you out of rehab. You know, write stuff down about all of them. Do the whole 'fearless moral inventory' in the Fourth Step—write down in your Eighth Step the list of people you'd screwed over and make plans to, like, you know, say you were sorry or something when you got out. I was always pretty good in school. This stuff was a snap. Like somebody's fifth-grade homework!

"And I was, you know, younger than just about anybody else. I thought this put me ahead. I mean, all these other old guys had wasted most of their lives. I still had my life ahead of me. I knew I'd *cured* myself, man. I was ready to go back to college, you know, be a model student, ace everything, get a great job, start running the world. Sure, I'd go to Twelve Step meetings. Meetings were okay. Might even meet some nice women at them. Never liked women who drank or drugged anyway. . . ."

Convinced he was "cured," Matt left rehab, went to a few meetings, and felt he knew more than anybody else. "I'd already done all the Twelve Steps in a month, for Chrissake, and there were people in the rooms been in the program for years who still hadn't done the Fourth Step!" Then, thrown by the first unanticipated bad feeling he had, Matt remembered the "Let go" part of "Let go, let God" and let himself pick up crack.

Within a week he was worse off than he'd ever been.

He quickly spent what money he had on drugs; then, broke, he thought about robbing people again. "I'd thrown away the first switchblade I had," Matt says. "So I had to go to the pawn shop to pick up another. I'd turned right back into the old zombie: I'd do anything to get high. But—I don't know. Something about looking at those blades got to me. What the fuck was I doing? I started to feel like shit again. Who knows what old lady was gonna get in my way this time?" Matt doesn't know where these unexpected pangs of conscience came from. He only knows he was somehow able to heed them when they hit. "It was like something jolted me awake. I don't know what it was. Maybe what they tell me is my Higher Power." Whatever it was, Matt felt like he "woke up" in the pawn shop and managed to steer himself back to his old detox and rehab.

We gave rage some pretty extensive coverage before, because it's so common to the experience of addicts and alcoholics. But so many other feelings can throw an addict and alcoholic. When Matt thinks back to when he decided to pick up crack again, he remembers exactly how he felt—a whole range of feelings, and rage was only one of them. "It's like it didn't matter what I felt," Matt says. "Even if I was happy—I'd get, like, *too* happy—like some kind of thunderstorm would start to build up inside me until I couldn't stand it. Or I'd get so bored I'd be ready to do anything to break the feeling. Or so sad, thinking of how I'd screwed myself up, thinking how I don't have any friends anymore because I can't hang around my old drug contacts and I don't feel comfortable yet with anybody in the rooms—you know, I'd get so sad I couldn't stand it."

Matt felt he wasn't safe from *any* feeling. But he's learning since coming back from his slip that even when his feelings make him miserable, they eventually break on their own and change into something else. And he can survive it. "I guess, before, I was acting like I'd die if I didn't *do* something to change my feeling. Now I realize I won't die. I'll just feel a certain way for a while, and then feel another way." Matt laughs. "Do I sound like a moron? I mean, do regular people think about this kind of stuff?" He shrugs. "I guess it doesn't matter. What matters is that I've started to figure out that if I just hang on for a while, things will change on their own. I don't always have to go out there and *do* anything to blow things up. Except, go to meetings. And maybe follow some suggestions. . . ."

Matt has a group of friends he goes out with for coffee after several meetings each week. For the first time he actually feels he's not alone—something he'd heard in meetings might be possible, but never really felt in his gut until recently. "My friends show me something I didn't know before. They let me know that I don't have to win any prizes in AA or NA. In fact, they say, hey, stay back a few grades. Keep going to the First Step—the one where you admit you're powerless over drugs and alcohol and that your life has become unmanageable—every time you get the idea that you're smarter than everybody else." Matt laughs again. "I used to hate it when people wished me a slow recovery. Now I guess I don't want it any other way. I need time, man. I can't do all this at once. I'm tired of trying to be Superman."

Having Feelings, Not Being Them

If there's one main revelation that all the people you've met so far in this book have reached, it's that *you can tolerate feelings without acting on them.* This is astonishing news to so many recovering people, people who have spent their lives reacting to feelings as if they were a chaotic pile of red-hot coals.

"I always felt like a turtle," says Sharon, a recovering addict with ten months of sobriety. "The least threat, and *zap*, back into my shell. Where, in the old days, I kept a fully stocked pharmacy." Now that the "pharmacy" has been emptied, Sharon is getting the courage to keep her head out of her "shell" a little longer, open her eyes a little wider. And she's slowly discovering that it's possible to experience the World Out There without descending into a state of abject terror.

"I've had to learn everything from scratch," admits Sharon, who has worked for a number of years as a freelance editor. "It's been very humbling. Because for so long, I'd pretended I knew everything—and sometimes I almost convinced myself I *did*. I could name-drop with the best of them. I'd had a few glamorous jobs as an editor early on with a number of conspicuous successes, big bestsellers. God, I milked *those* for all they were worth. I left the company I was with just before they were about to discreetly suggest that perhaps I'd be happier elsewhere; I hadn't gotten any of my books in on time for a couple of years, and those that got through were disasters. But I had it announced in all the trade papers that I was going freelance. One magazine even did an interview with me: I went on endlessly about my 'need for freedom.' Truth was, I couldn't hold down a job in a company anymore. But I rode on my early stellar reputation for years. And it worked, for a while. I mean, when I was on Valium and other downs, I did everything I could to convey this image of total competence. 'No problem,' I'd say about anything to anyone. And frankly, I often believed myself. If you were as 'mellow' as I regularly got on drugs, you wouldn't have thought anything was a problem either! People would buy into it for a while too. Who doesn't like to hear that there's 'no problem'? But then, inevitably, they wouldn't get the work they commissioned from me on time. I became positively ingenious with excuses. But even those wore off. I lost client after client. And one day I got so doped up nearly killed myself."

Sharon sighs. "It's been a long way back. Now that I've been through an outpatient clinic, and I'm going to NA meetings, I'm in a whole new world. As I said, I realize I have to learn everything from scratch. How to buy food sensibly at a supermarket, for example. How to vacuum my apartment!" Sharon laughs. "For years, every so often I'd call in some expensive cleaning service and they'd send some poor crew over who would gasp at the mess I'd made of my home and work for two days to clean it up. Now I can't afford them, and I'm having to learn to take care of myself. I'll never forget the first time I actually found myself scrubbing my kitchen floor, on my hands and knees. I wanted to call in the neighbors and say, 'Look what I've done!' It was a big triumph for me. It still is."

Slowly, Sharon is beginning to establish herself as an editor again, taking on smaller projects, projects she feels she can handle in these early, baffling days of sobriety. "At first I couldn't *read* anything; a big liability when you're an editor! Now I can read and actually edit articles and book proposals. Maybe, who knows, someday I can get to the big stuff."

Recently an old client, from what Sharon calls her "grandiose" days, called and invited her out to dinner at an expensive restaurant to talk to her about a "really big" job. Sharon knew she wasn't ready for something too taxing, but she was intrigued.

"God, it was weird," she says. "This was the ex-president of a major company who'd bounced around from publishing company to publishing company for years—not an uncommon occurrence in the book business, but I saw, now that I was sober, one of the major reasons *why* he'd never been able to stay in one place. He was a roaring alcoholic."

Sharon found herself far more fascinated by how her dinner companion was acting than by any "business" he was allegedly there to conduct. "It was quickly clear that the dinner was an excuse for him to write off yet another meeting on his current publisher's expense account. Which basically meant he got to drink as much as he wanted to for free. It was amazing watching him. I never really drank all that much when I was 'out there'; pills were my drug of choice. But I did downs, so I knew the zonked-out state this guy was feeling, the escape he was after. And that's what was so strange, fascinating, and sad. Moving, even. The more he drank, the more childlike he became. I felt I was in some clinical laboratory watching him. He made these associative leaps, just like a little child does, not able to hold one thought for longer than a moment, quickly moving on to the next feeling or thought. Inhibitions washed out of him with each glass of wine. He spilled out his marital troubles; he was on the verge of a divorce. Nobody understood him. Which reminded him of a trip he wanted to take to Venice. Or was it Corfu? Oh, who knew. He did love to travel. Didn't I? Yes, we should really work on a travel book together. Perhaps a travel novel, yes, that would be lovely. Maybe, to hell with it, we'd stop being editors and write it ourselves. Who knew more about writing than two old pros like us? And by the way, was I sure I didn't want a drink? Why was I so quiet? I really was so much more fun when I had a few drinks. . . .

"What struck me most was that he was so desperately trying to escape any pain—and desperately, if barely consciously, seeking to make contact with someone. He seemed like one of the loneliest people I'd ever met. And I identified—*God*, how I identified with him! How alone I felt when I was still drugging and drinking! I was convinced no one, no one at all, could ever understand what I was going through." Sharon frowns. "I'm still not saying what moved me most, though. It's just this: My terribly drunk dinner companion reminded me that I'm after exactly the same thing now that I was when I drugged and drank—a feeling that I'm *all right*. A feeling of oneness with the world. Self-acceptance. The ability to stay in my own skin. An escape from hating myself. An escape from fear. The ability to tolerate life— to enjoy it. Or, in Bill Wilson's words, to be '*happy, joyous, and free.*'" Sharon closes her eyes for a moment, then opens them; her face is full of new light. "That's the revelation. I saw this poor drunken guy trying, vainly, to do what I am starting to be able to do sober: accept and get comfortable with my feelings. With who I am. All the pills I was taking weren't the answer, though, God knows, I tried to make them be. This guy, still drinking, hadn't learned what I was now sure was true: Drinking wasn't going to give him the peace he was after. All drinking could do was make him drunk. Sever him from himself. *Keep* him from being who he wanted to be."

Bombing out on downs hadn't ever helped Sharon to attain the sense of self-acceptance and serenity she now realized she'd always been after and also now realized she at least had a chance of attaining, sober. "What began as a way to get rid of my inhibitions—zonking myself out with drugs—ended in paralysis," Sharon said. "I see now that I took pills because I was so desperate to feel good about myself, but they never really helped, even if, for a while, I thought they did. All that ever happened was that vacant, childlike, transient state I'd seen in my drunken friend. The pills were only a cover-up. But so was any attempt to find self-acceptance or self-esteem in my job. Even when, in the early days, I had my big professional successes, nothing really touched me deep inside; nothing really made it easier to accept who I was."

The "small" triumphs Sharon can lay claim to today—cleaning her home, buying groceries, taking on manageable projects and getting them done when she says she'll get them done—these are all immensely more gratifying to her than any flashier success in her drugged past. She now feels, she says, "at least a glimmer of the serenity my drunken friend and I were starving for, out of it on booze or drugs. It's a real serenity. Something that comes out of *who I am*. Not some ephemeral 'feel-good' state temporarily imposed on me by a drug, by something external. I've earned what little serenity I feel. I'm developing it, cultivating it in myself. And it's real—in fact, all of my feelings are real—in a way no other emotional state ever was before. I can cherish, depend on, *allow* feelings to enrich my life and make me open to more and more things. Less apt to retreat back into the old shell."

This is the ideal, anyway. Sharon admits that she still panics; she still feels overwhelmed by life, by the swings of her moods, by sudden doubts about her future, fears about whether she'll be able to continue her professional ascent, confusion about just who she "really" is now that she's not losing herself in drugs. But already, helped in a strange way by seeing how lost her intoxicated dinner companion seemed, she's begun to see, as many people begin to see in their first year of sobriety, that self-acceptance might after all be possible in sobriety. The instinct for self-preservation, the fierce desire to *live*, not die, that seems to characterize many addicts' and alcoholics' first moments of recovery, is one that can be nurtured, cultivated, brought to bloom. The "flower" is a feeling of genuine self-acceptance, the knowledge, the *certainty* that feelings don't have to be toxic. Feelings are a kind of mental weather that will eventually pass and change into something else, not something you get trapped in forever. This is what is meant by "Feelings are not facts."

"I realize that saying 'I'm angry' when anger hits isn't precisely true." Sharon says. "It's truer to say 'I *feel* anger.' It's important for me to remind myself that I am not my anger; anger is a state I happen to be in, temporarily. Not that there might not be some very good reasons for being in that state, reasons that bear looking into. But my anger, or any other feeling I have, doesn't have to kill me. Or make me pick up a drug."

It's the experience of so many recovering people that sobriety breeds flexibility. The more sober we become, the more difficult it is to categorize ourselves in any rigid way. Once again, Sharon illuminates: "I used to think I was the type of person who never, oh, I don't know—liked baseball, say. Or who would never get peeved when somebody cut in front of me in line at the grocery store; I was always too mellow to be bothered by anything so petty. Now, sober, I'm finding I do sort of like baseball. In fact, I was ready to hurl a few baseballs at this pushy woman at the market the other day who barged in front of me in line!" Sharon, like many other recovering people, is discovering she isn't a "type" after all. She's capable of any number of responses, and capable of feeling any number of emotions.

A big lesson that Sharon helps to teach us is simply this: We don't have to *become* our feelings. Important as feelings can be as signals, markers that tell us what's going on inside, we come to realize that feelings are not "facts," especially as we allow ourselves to witness their coming and going. "This too shall pass" may be, at different times, the most exasperating and the most reassuring slogan you'll hear at Twelve Step meetings. What it seems to remain, however, is *true*. The only constant in sobriety (or in life) seems to be that however you're feeling now isn't how you'll be feeling tomorrow. Or later today. Or in a moment.

But something beneath this doesn't change quite so precipitously. At least, this is what recovering people who've got a few months of sobriety under their belts tell me. As we allow ourselves to *witness* our feelings (rather than identify ourselves completely with them), we seem eventually to become aware of a deeper "river" beneath all our surface emotional turmoil—a sort of calm, reliable, deep flow of serenity that doesn't go away, no matter what's happening back up there at the surface. We learn, in fact, that we can always come back to this subterranean flow for sustenance and direction and peace. Making contact with this river seems to be an organic consequence of sobriety. We seem to give ourselves the best chance of sensing it as we allow ourselves to experience feelings without judging them, allow what we feel to come out, whether in a trickle or in a torrent—all the while hanging on to our decision that, no matter what, *we don't have to pick up a drug or a drink.* This river of serenity seems to make itself felt too, when we reinforce our decision not to drink or drug by doing something we know from experience is positive, such as going to a Twelve Step meeting, making a phone call to another recovering person, or doing something else we know will bolster our decision to stay sober. We learn from all of this to "hang on" so that we can truly "let go" of feelings that seem to assail us, that *seem* as if they would put us under. We learn they don't have to. We've got options—not the least of which is simply waiting until whatever feeling is tormenting us passes.

It's clear to me from talking to people in recovery that these revelations about feelings don't all come at the same time or rate or as completely for some people as they do for others. Often the only thing that makes sense to any of us in the first year of sobriety is that reliable standby: "Don't drink. Go to meetings." But, perhaps in a quiet moment, you may begin to feel the deep flow of that "river" I've described, and realize, as Sharon realized, that you're cultivating more peace of mind and self-acceptance than you ever thought you could before. Consciousness of this flow seems to increase the longer we stay sober. As you begin to work the Twelve Steps and keep renewing the pact with yourself not to drink or drug, the pull of that serenity deep within you can't seem to help but get stronger.

However, don't worry if all you can feel right now is the turmoil on top. In fact, dealing with that turmoil constitutes a very important aim for everyone who grapples with sobriety, no matter how long they've been sober. Staying sober is a day-to-day (sometimes minute-to-minute) process with some very practical realities. We'll begin to get a sense of them in the next chapter. For example, how do you fill all the *time* you've got now that you're not filling it with alcohol or drugs or other ways of "acting out"? What have other people in their first year of sobriety learned about this? How have they learned to change their attitudes about structuring their days and nights? It's fine to say "first things first," or "do the next right thing." But how do you figure out what the "first" or "next right" thing is?

The people you'll meet in the next chapter should help you with these nuts-and-bolts questions about sobriety. And they can give you hope, if you need it, that taking even the smallest steps in a new direction can bring a whole new view into focus, one that's a hell of a lot more rewarding than the view you get from a bar stool.

four

Sitcoms and Mashed Potatoes:
Managing Time, Sober

I owe a great debt of gratitude to mashed potatoes. Also to TV reruns of *The Jeffersons, Gimme a Break,* and *Benson,* and the local seven o'clock news. They all helped me stay sober.

Like most of the people we've met in this book, I experienced early sobriety as a revelation, a mostly positive one. Physical changes were amazing and unexpectedly gratifying. My chronic diarrhea stopped. I learned the joys of sleeping as opposed to the "relief" of passing out. Suddenly the world seemed to have so much more color in it: Even my sight seemed to get better.

What didn't at first get better was my sense of what the hell to do with myself. Now that I'd decided not to spend every available moment in pursuit of alcohol, I suddenly had all this *time.* How was I supposed to spend it? I had a vague notion it was time to be productive in some "normal" way, but the prospect alternately baffled, bored, and terrified me. I couldn't imagine how to do it.

I'd always wondered how "normal" people got that way. That umpteenth bleary-eyed morning after the bars and after-hours clubs had closed, on yet another day I'd decided to take off from work, I'd squint painfully at people in business suits striding off to their offices. How did they manage it? They looked so alive, clean, purposeful—normal. I hated them. Sometimes I'd try to feel superior: I was just too artistic, sensitive, iconoclastic, wise, worldly to buy into the "normal" world they were part of. Being conventional meant being dull. And I had a horror of ever being that.

But secretly I envied them. They'd figured out something I hadn't. They seemed to have some idea where they were going. I was convinced that whatever it was that enabled them to make money, save money, pay bills, keep lovers and spouses, take vacations, do their laundry—whatever that was, it was constitutionally lacking in me. When God put me together, he'd obviously left out some essential machinery.

Was it possible to acquire that "machinery" now? I didn't know. All I knew was that now that I wasn't drinking anymore, I had to face the problem of not feeling normal in a different way than I had before. No longer was I willing to use this discomfort as an excuse to get drunk ("To hell with the world, I wasn't meant for it; I'll just check out!"). I found myself willing to face, if, at first, unable to answer, a basic question about sober life: What do I do now that I'm not spending every possible moment getting high?

At first I did the only thing I knew how to do. I went back to my old bar. I shudder as I recount this now, knowing how easy it would have been to have asked the bartender to give me vodka instead of club soda, but I didn't appreciate the risks back then. The only people I knew went to bars. I couldn't imagine being comfortable anywhere else. So why couldn't I just go back, but not drink alcohol?

I found out why all too soon. Bars, when you don't get drunk in them, are boring. I watched with a kind of clinical fascination as old "friends" descended, drink by drink, into various degrees of stupor. Endlessly repeated stories, stupid jokes, maudlin protestations of love and devotion, gratuitous nastiness, and then, finally, the blank-eyed "nobody's home but us chickens" expression that precedes passing out into an ashtray. It got through even my dense head: I had no place in bars anymore. I had to find something else.

So I tried something radically new: I actually went home after work. It was amazing how exotic this seemed! Finding my sitcom reruns and the evening news, knowing that any number of people were watching the same stuff in their own homes at the same time, was almost exhilarating. I don't know where I got the idea of mashing potatoes; I guess it was the most "normal" food I could think of. But I have a vivid memory of standing in the kitchen, looking out at the TV in the next room, mashing potatoes I'd bought and boiled myself in my very own pot, pleasantly watching George Jefferson go through his paces. It was somehow both cleansing and magical. I'd discovered for the first time something, I've since learned, many other recovering people discover with equal amazement: *I could do what other people did. And even enjoy it.* Maybe I wasn't so different after all. Maybe it was okay, at least for the moment, to be "ordinary." Normal. Not scrabbling about for one more fantastic outta-sight high. Maybe I could just simply *be.* Live with all my senses open, unaltered. Mashing potatoes became an extraordinary experience. It was something I could do with complete calm. I found a different, deeper satisfaction pounding away at a potato than I'd ever experienced pounding down shots of vodka.

Highlights of my day though they were, sitcoms and mashed potatoes couldn't take up all my time. There were all those hours before 5:00 P.M. and after 7:30 P.M. to get through too. Figuring out how to structure this time has taken guidance and practice. It has meant tripping over myself, making mistakes, trying out things that didn't always work, experiencing panic and confusion and sometimes wonder at the new, clearer life I found and find myself living sober. Sometimes I've overbooked myself, sometimes underbooked. But the guidance I've received from people who'd been here before me and had made similar stumbling progress has been invaluable. It's taught me something crucial, something I've observed most recovering people seem to catch onto sooner or later: *No one knows automatically how to do things,* how to live "productively." No one is born knowing how to open a bank account or balance a checkbook, do taxes, ride a bike, drive a car, go to the dry cleaner's, stand in line in a supermarket, hook up a vcr, run a computer, screw in a light bulb, have a give-and-take conversation on the telephone. We all have to *learn* these things, to learn how to live.

Maybe this sounds obvious. But how many times have you pretended you knew something because you were too embarrassed or ashamed to say that you didn't? Many of us would sooner turn inside out than admit we don't know how to do something we think we "ought" to know how to do. As one twenty-five-year-old recovering addict told me, "I grew up telling my parents 'Let me make my own mistakes!' as a way of avoiding following their or anybody else's advice. I couldn't stand anyone telling me what to do, or even making a suggestion. As a result, I don't know how to do anything!"

The hard truth I had to face in my first days and months of sobriety was simply this: I hadn't learned some pretty basic things. The comforting truth was that I wasn't alone: Other recovering people were as much in the dark about how to live as I was. But that didn't stop them. They made daily stabs at living, humbling first steps toward figuring out how to get from A to B to C, stuff they believed that everyone was "supposed" to know, but that they'd somehow missed. They kept trying even when, at first, things didn't work out. They looked and asked for guidance and found it.

Let's meet some of these people right now and see what I mean.

Trials and Errors: Building a Sober Life

Jamaica laughs from somewhere deep inside her, a great rich wave rumbling up. "It's like this, honey. I'm a fat, black, blind-in-one eye, gay, forty-five-year-old female alcoholic and drug addict. Not most likely to be your next president. Though heaven knows," she sighs theatrically, "this country could use me." One thing, Jamaica insists, had always been true about her: "I never needed nuthin' from nobody. You could take your advice and stick it where the moon don't shine." Jamaica's eyes are full of humor; she's goofing on herself, a little.

"At least," she continues, "that's the Jamaica that used to be. And sometimes still is. I mean, I still think most people are jerks. But this damned recovery stuff keeps cutting me down to what I keep hearing is my 'right size.' I keep having to realize that, okay, maybe I'm not impenetrable and omniscient. Maybe I still have some stuff to learn. . . .

"I grew up different, feeling different, acting different. Wouldn't take no shit from nobody. Smarter than everybody else. And knew I was gay forever. Made no secret I loved women. People around me thought I was deranged." Abandoned as a teenager by her family, who she collectively "horrifies," Jamaica perfected her defensive, challenging stance in order to survive. "I learned to fight dirty," she says. "You pull out a knife, you got a broken arm." Her blindness is the result of one of the few fights she lost, a brutal melee at fifteen with a drunken cousin who, in the course of trying to rape her, hit her with a baseball bat.

Jamaica escaped the violence and restrictions of her childhood to create, she said, "new violence and restrictions—with sex, drugs, alcohol, and a string of loser drug addict whores I couldn't seem to stop falling for." But Jamaica had ambitions beyond the ghetto life. Somehow, despite the hell she lived in, returning to various fleabag SRO hotels with whatever "down-and-out back-stabbing bitch" she happened to be involved with at the moment, she got a high school equivalency diploma. Mainly on the spoils of drug deals, she was putting herself through college at night. She discovered something interesting: She had a real flair for writing poetry. "I was a tough street mutha," Jamaica said, "with poetry teachers who thought they'd found a rose growing out of concrete. Well," she says with some pride, "they *had.*" Jamaica led a double life between what she calls "pale white spectacled wimps and librarian-types oohing and aahing over my 'powerful' poems—some of them would have given me an A for farting, I think—" and "Charlene or Jolene or whatever other 'ene I happened to be screwing around with back in the ghetto, dealing and doing drugs, having horrendous jealous knock-down fights, all of which would seep into my poetry and get me more A's and oohs and aahs from my professors . . ." Jamaica shakes her head. "It wore me down."

When one of Jamaica's love spats nearly resulted in murder—"the police walked in just as I pulled out the kitchen knife, and I woulda used it too"—she ended up, drunk, in a detox and a rehab, and found that she was ready to "surrender." Recovery took hold because, as Jamaica says, "I was too tired to hold onto anything else." She began to get better. "I left my thieving whore of a 'lover' when I got out of rehab, and a college professor found me a cheap room in a better part of town. I was determined to live a new life."

But Jamaica felt like a steamroller without anything to steamroll. "I loved not being drunk and strung out all the time. But all I'd ever known was screwing around and getting high and fighting. I didn't have a clue how to live without doing all that stuff." At first, Jamaica threw herself into AA and NA "service," setting up chairs at meetings, making coffee, filling her life with "program." "I was gonna do a complete turnaround. Become Saint Jamaica. They'd build shrines to this selfless black woman, this incredible lady poet/goddess whose life had become a shining inspiration to all. . . ." Jamaica groans softly. "I was somehow both bored out of my mind and fed up to here with being busy. All this goddamn busy-ness—like a bee with no hive. I kept buzzing around, not feeling really at home anywhere. I missed the partying. The wild, let-it-loose sex and getting high. The fights. God, I loved to fight! But I didn't think I could talk about that stuff with my recovering friends. Hell, they didn't seem like friends yet. They seemed like, I don't know, sister inmates. We were all pussyfooting around being sweet and nice and goody-goody. 'Care for some coffee?' 'Here, let me move my chair over so you'll have more room.' 'Want me to open the window so you're comfortable?' Sober life was a tea party from hell."

Jamaica started, she says, "finding myself roaming the old neighborhood. I bumped into one of my old lovers hawking her ass on the corner. Had to admit, she looked good. She said, 'Hey, Jamaica, where you *been*, honey?'" Jamaica pauses for a moment, then shrugs. "You know how, when you die, you're supposed to see your life go whizzing in front of your eyes? Well, that's sort of what happened then. Got these flashes of brightly lit rooms and goody-two-shoes, boring recovering addicts and alcoholics, buzzing out on the coffee, politely stranding themselves in doorways saying 'you first, no *you* first, no *you* first,' like those damned cartoon chipmunks—and here was this hot lady wondering where I'd been. Tell the truth, *I* wondered where I'd been too—and why."

Jamaica reached reflexively for the flask of cheap whiskey she knew "Charlene" had in her shoulder bag, took it out, unscrewed it, and almost took a swig. "But then, in just as quick a flash, the other half of my life came back. The blood and the anger and hell and the hangovers and feeling like shit . . ." Somehow Jamaica managed to screw the top back onto the flask, smile at her lady friend, and say, "I been getting better, honey. See you around." And she willed herself to turn and walk away.

Jamaica isn't entirely comfortable admitting the next part. "I trembled. I was scared. I was so close to screwing things up again. And damn, I didn't want to do that. I really don't want to go back to hell. But I wasn't this strong Saint Jamaica anymore. I was a trembling little girl. A little girl I'd never allowed myself to be before." Jamaica went to a nearby AA meeting that was already in progress. "I felt I was starving for it, now. My fellow 'inmates' didn't seem so goody-goody anymore. They seemed as needy as I was. They were here because they'd been elsewhere and here was better. I made a vow at that moment that I'd try to learn how to fill my time sober, not just be busy, but try for something that felt right, something that wouldn't capsize me."

She began listening to people who talked about being bored in sobriety, or maniacally busy, or happy in having found ways to restructure their lives. She'd always felt superior to much of the program literature, but she found herself picking up a copy of AA's *Living Sober* and reading it in a new way. Now it seemed less a list of schoolteacher do's and don'ts than suggestions based on hard-earned experience of recovering people. People who'd grappled with the same unwieldiness of time she now struggled with in sobriety. "Most of the stuff I'm learning is common sense," Jamaica says. "Like avoid bars. Schedule your day around meetings. Stay away from anything that threatens your sobriety." The phrase "people, places, and things" has begun for Jamaica to seem less a catchphrase than a useful warning: She now sees that it is precisely the quality of people, places, and things that has the greatest bearing on her sobriety and her life.

Jamaica is also discovering that she can ask questions about all of this and admit that she doesn't know what she doesn't know. "That's the biggest change," she says today, ten months sober. "I always was the lady who knew it all, had seen it all, and didn't need to consult anybody about anything. Now that my life is changing—I've got a part-time job at the college library to supplement a scholarship I also just got, and they've got these goddamn computers there and what the fuck do I know about computers—anyway, I'm slowing down, and taking a deep breath, and asking to be taught what I don't know." Trial and error, giving herself permission to make mistakes, finding out what's too busy and what's not busy enough, what's meaningful and what isn't, who really *are* the "winners" she's supposed to "stick with" in sobriety: All of this is part of the "Great Lesson" Jamaica says she is slowly, humbly, allowing herself to learn.

"Getting off alcohol and drugs—you know, that's just the beginning," Jamaica sums up. "I need to learn how to live life. That's the hard part. Because if I can't work that out, there won't be any reason not to go back to drinking and drugging. I didn't get sober to be miserable. So, God help me to get a life I can live, that I want to live. And that I won't have to turn into Mother Teresa to pull it off. Two slogans I used to think were stupid now save my ass. 'Keep it simple,' and 'One day at a time.' Amazing what those words can do to calm me down, how they can help me see what, really, I ought to be looking at, right now."

Sanity over Sainthood: Sorting Out Priorities in Sobriety

Though many alcoholics and addicts have an overwhelming sense of time when they first get sober, they don't always feel that it's a vast desert to be filled in new, "productive" ways. Some newly sober people's schedules seem to fill themselves up so quickly that they can't imagine how, in the past, they ever managed to find the time to drink or drug.

Philip, at thirty-two, is soft-spoken but intense; he gives the accurate impression of being superorganized and efficient. Slightly balding, his light blond hair beginning to gray, the serious expression in his bespectacled blue eyes and brow seemingly a permanent imprint, he looks a bit, perhaps, like one of Jamaica's "librarian-type" poetry professors. Certainly his background and life situation couldn't be more different than Jamaica's. The only child of God-fearing, alcohol-shunning parents in a small midwestern town, Philip got all the benefits

˙(some of them, he says, "questionable") of a small, insulated, tightly knit family.

His drinking, he says, was "pure rebellion," although carried out with great discretion, like his very few other rebellions (eating potato chips in bed; smoking cigarillos in the basement). He managed to get through a small traditional college with respectable B's, all the while keeping more-or-less happily (if quietly) drunk with his frat brothers. "My only positive reputation," Philip says, "was that I could drink more than anybody else and not show it. Of course one of the reasons I didn't show it is that drinking made me sit in a corner and not say anything. God knows what they would have thought if I'd managed to stand up or try to talk. . . ."

Philip got a job in the library of his college after he graduated because he was "too terrified to go away. College was all I knew, all I could imagine living in." He took great pains to hide his drinking, buying and consuming cases of beer after work and on weekends, driving hung over at dawn on Monday morning to cart his considerable refuse of empty cans to a town dump forty miles away "to get rid of the evidence." In the meantime he compulsively kept up with work, forcing himself, whatever his physical state ("all of my waking life not drinking was a hangover"), to be reliable, on time, as productive as a well-tuned machine. While he managed quite successfully to hide the tension between his drunken time off and his white-knuckled "public" life at work, it gnawed away at him inside. In fact, Philip gradually descended into a state of desperation and loneliness so deep that he became suicidal. Secretly, surreptitiously scanning relevant sources in the library computer, he began to research various "clean," painless ways of killing himself.

Then, suddenly, he met someone he called his "savior": Annmarie. Annmarie, a few years older than Philip, was a divorced teaching assistant at the college who, for some reason, fixated on him as husband material ("Maybe," he speculates, "she thought I was responsible because I was so quiet.") Annmarie's previous husband had been a womanizing drunk. Little did she realize that her second husband-to-be was just as much of a drunk, even if he'd never had the nerve to be a womanizer.

Philip was as intoxicated by Annmarie's attentions as he was by his nightly beer drinking. "I'd barely had three dates in college, which you couldn't exactly call successes. I sat in front of each girl in the frat living room and poured us beer all night. Don't think we talked much. Mostly I sat there with a stupid grin on my face." Annmarie, however, didn't seem put off by Philip's marked lack of social skills. She was "forthright" and "strong," and she "knew what she wanted—which somehow," Philip said, "was me." Philip felt swept away; they married within months of meeting each other.

Unfortunately, however, marriage didn't put a dent in Philip's drinking; it just made it harder to hide. "The despair came back. Being married to Annmarie soon just made me feel like more of a failure. I couldn't seem to be the successful, ambitious man she wanted. Which only made me want to drink more." Annmarie discovered Philip's hidden cases of beer in the basement and was furious. She wasn't going to put up with another alcoholic in her life, and she delivered an ultimatum: "Either I got help or she wanted a divorce." Somewhat against his will, Philip entered therapy and began going to AA, where he's been for nearly eleven months, now quite a bit less against his will.

"I resisted AA at first. I wasn't going for myself at first; I was going to hang on to my marriage. But the main thing was, it just seemed like more *stuff* I had to do. I already felt overwhelmed by the details of my job, by trying to be a model husband, and, when I was drinking, by trying to keep up my drinking while hiding it. Suddenly, now, I had to replace drinking with something just as time-consuming: doing all these Steps, reading all this literature. That's, anyway, what I thought in the beginning." Philip's response to any new task was to "psyche it out and determine the quickest, most efficient way of getting it done. I figured I could enter the main points from the Big Book and AA's *Twelve Steps and Twelve Traditions* into the computer, make some time charts—like, plan so many days on the First Step, talk to the college chaplain about God so I'd be ready for the Second Step, you know, maybe do a little backup reading in theology to prepare for the Third Step, then consult sources like *The One Minute Manager* for the least time-consuming and most effective way to organize and produce my 'fearless moral inventory' in the Fourth Step. . . ." Philip attacked "program" with the same conscientious zeal he brought to his work as a librarian. It didn't take him long to echo Jamaica: "I was worn out."

Then, about a month ago, his wife announced the unthinkable: She told him she was pregnant. "I really freaked out," Philip said. "Here I was, struggling to get sober and do the program perfectly and be a perfect husband and worker and now—my God—I had to be a father too?" Philip's days were already crammed full in sobriety; he worked extra hours to make more money so that Annmarie would think he was ambitious; made the coffee and cleaned up afterward at his daily AA meetings; volunteered to organize various events at his church. He was averaging about five hours of sleep a night. "When did I ever have time to drink? And now how will I ever have time to be a father?"

Philip could think of only one escape: drinking. But he had the courage to talk about it at AA meetings. People at meetings seemed to pick up on what was really bothering him and making him want to drink: He was trying too hard to be perfect at everything, including recovery. One woman talked about her own compulsive attempts to be "the best, most efficient recovering person in history," and how she was learning it was okay to let up on herself. Philip thought about it. He had a couple of weeks of vacation coming up, which he'd originally planned to spend doing work on the house, planning the summer church picnic, completing any number of other chores and self-imposed obligations. But maybe, just this once, he'd plan some time away with Annmarie instead: two weeks at the seashore.

Annmarie surprised him by leaping at the chance to get away; she was tired of her own grind as a teaching assistant, and full of anxiety herself at becoming a parent. Time off right now would be perfect, she thought. And so, with his usual conscientiousness, Philip found and booked a small cottage at just the right bend of beach in just the right nearby coastal resort for just the right amount of money. "Everything in its place, puts a smile on my face!" was one of his mother's admonitions, and Philip was his mother's son, so packing took most of the day; packing the car took most of another. Finally they were on their way. Finally they got there. Finally they unpacked.

And then, as Philip puts it, "I was faced with the awful terror of two blank weeks." Dutifully, he helped Annmarie pack a picnic lunch; gloomily he dragged a food hamper and blanket and umbrella and towel down to the seashore on a grimly perfect cloudless blue day. He spread all of his belongings carefully down on the sand and sat. He was hit by a sense of misery so strong it almost made him physically sick. There was nothing he hated more than nothing to do. How was he gong to survive the "vacation"?

But then, suddenly, he was hit by something else. A spray of sand and water grittily assailed him as if his own private cyclone had spun out of the ocean. Astonished, he found himself face-to-face with a panting golden retriever. He looked around in panic: Whose dog was this? Nobody was near their blanket; nobody seemed to be looking for a dog. The dog, rather, seemed to have decided that Philip was his owner. He pawed at Philip, whimpering, then ran over to a well-chewed stick. He barked. It was clear what the dog had in mind—if not to the astonished Philip, then at least to the dog and Annmarie. Annmarie laughed. "He wants to *play*," she said. Philip looked at her helplessly. "Oh, go ahead," she laughed, pushing at him. "Throw him his stick!" So Philip wobbled up to his feet, grabbed the stick, and gave it a halfhearted toss toward the surf.

The dog went crazy. "I've never seen a creature so full of *joy*," Philip remembers. "It was like I'd done the thing he'd been waiting for his whole life, the most perfect thing anyone could have done for him: toss a stick." The retriever richly lived up to the promise of his breed, and brought the stick back, wagging himself into a frenzy, awaiting the next delicious throw, hardly able to contain himself with the excitement of it all. "I began to laugh a little. Dopey dog. I threw the stick with a little more force now. It went out just beyond the foam of the surf, and the dog leapt in after it, first losing it in the white bubbling water, then finding it with the greatest enthusiasm. . . ."

At the end of an hour, Philip had become a bounding Ichabod Crane, as wet and sandy as the dog, laughing and unwieldy in the breaking surf, even stopping for a moment to sit in it (getting sand in his swimming trunks in the bargain), resting while he hugged the golden retriever by his side, the two creatures in a happy unthinking bond. "Annmarie said we looked like a dog and his boy!" Philip laughs, today. "But it was incredible; I'd never felt like this before. Something in me totally released. I'd never *run* before! I'd never just—played with anyone, anything, any creature like I was playing with this new friend. And somehow the best thing was I didn't care about myself; I didn't care how I looked, running, throwing a stick—I wasn't *embarrassed* about it! I'd lost all self-consciousness. It was okay to be messy, clumsy, do nothing but have fun. It was like some whole new self got born in me. And I wasn't even drunk!"

The dog's true owner finally did turn up: Philip said he felt like crying when the dog was taken away. But he also felt transformed. "Even Annmarie could see the difference. From that moment on, it actually became possible to have a real vacation. I relaxed somewhere deep inside me. I wasn't compulsively looking around for the next 'correct' thing to do." Luckily, in his conscientiousness, Philip had chosen a resort with an active AA group right in town; he went to a meeting that night with a real sense of pleasure and eagerness to share the new feelings he'd discovered within himself.

Two weeks later, when he and Annmarie returned to their workaday world, with Philip astonished that he could feel so refreshed, he found himself approaching AA and his job and even the prospect of parenthood differently. "It's not that my compulsiveness has magically disappeared. Sometimes I get antsy and perfectionistic and crazy. But I'm able to remember the dog most times and calm down." He's also managed to cut back on his obligations, "sorting out in my heart as well as my mind what I really need or want to do. Giving myself *time*, in other words, to sit with different possibilities and choose, more calmly and purposefully, the course I really want to take—not the course some reflexive guilt tells me I 'should' be taking."

The sense that we've got to be perfect or do things perfectly in order to be even marginally acceptable is a pervasive one for recovering people, particularly for newly recovering people who, like Philip and Jamaica and so many others, want so desperately to "get it right" after making such a mess of their drinking and drugging lives. The problem is that this quest for perfection almost always turns into a kind of self-attack: inevitably we find imperfections in ourselves, endless ways we're *not* "getting it right," and we feel a deepening of self-mistrust, even self-hate, instead of the lifting of negativity we're hoping for in recovery.

It seems crucial to be as patient and compassionate with yourself as you can be. Changing something as deeply bred as your dependency on drugs or alcohol (or any other escape-hatch behaviors you used to cling to that have proven to be self-destructive) isn't easy. And as important as it is to be aware of "people, places, and things," avoiding any of them that threaten your sobriety as you take a new look at how you want to spend your time, sometimes you can't change that overnight, either. This is especially the case with the "people" part of "people, places, and things."

Witness Michael.

When You're a Drunk
(and So's Your Mother)

Michael can't remember a time when he didn't feel shame, up to and including his first few months of sobriety. "Maybe, it's my Irish Catholic guilt," he says. "The nuns really did do a number on me. But everyone says that, don't they? Catholic schools get such a bad rap. . . ." Michael's feelings of being "less than" were deep-rooted; his school experiences only compounded them. Overweight from childhood, asthmatic and shy, he was never a popular kid growing up in his neighborhood, a tough part of Chicago where only fists and the amount you could drink got you any respect. Michael was hopeless at fighting and, for a long time, morally opposed to drinking—"I was a real little prig, as a kid"—which made him pretty much of a pariah. This situation was not helped by the fact that his mother was an alcoholic who lived on welfare (Michael's alcoholic father had long ago died of cirrhosis) and was as shunned in the neighborhood as Michael. "Being on welfare meant you were scum in that Irish neighborhood," Michael said. "I was so ashamed of my mother, of her being a drunk and not having a job, of not having a father, of having no money." He sought some kind of refuge in his church, becoming an altar boy, helping out with this or that church activity, and self-hating as he was, he wasn't much more liked at church than he was anywhere else.

He remembers, at sixteen, making the decision to take his first drink. "I'd just gotten pushed down for the umpteenth time in front of our building by one of the neighborhood bullies. I climbed the stairs, humiliated as usual, hating myself more than

ever, and went into the bathroom to wash the dirt off my jacket.
I looked in the mirror and hated the fat, stupid face I saw staring
back at me. What did it matter what I did? All my family seemed
to be good for was drinking. So I went into my mother's bed-
room—she was already taking one of her 'naps,' which meant
she'd passed out again—and I took her half-empty bottle of cheap
whiskey, brought it into the kitchen, and poured myself a glass-
ful. I'd literally never had a drink before this; I'd barely allowed
myself to *smell* the communion wine in church, I'd only pretended to sip it, because I hated the thought of alcohol so much.
But now it was different. Now I was growing into my 'inheri-
tance.' I knew the truth, finally: I was just a drunk waiting to
happen. Why argue with fate? So, after choking the first glass
down—Lord, I can still feel that heave in my stomach when that
cheap rotgut stuff hit it—I felt almost, in a strange, depressed
way, *relieved.* I was on my way to becoming the only thing I had
a hope of being good at: a drunk."

It did indeed seem to Michael that he'd found his calling. Very
soon he understood why people drank. It really did make him feel
better. Or rather, eventually, it made him feel nothing, which was
even better than "better." "Problems just disappeared," Michael
says. "Booze was terrific. Everything it was cracked up to be."
During the next five, ten, fifteen years, Michael became more and
more accepted as the new neighborhood drunk. He and his
mother were, in fact, thought of almost as the neighborhood's
mascots; everybody made fun of them as one or the other
emerged from their squalid two-room apartment to get more
booze from the liquor store. They were fixtures, laughable oddi-
ties. "I worked a little, here and there, at first. I'd always done
well at school; with those nuns rapping you with rulers all the
time you almost had to do well! So I'd make reasonably good first
impressions at different jobs, here and there. Working as an office
file clerk, usually. Once I got a job in a florist's. But I couldn't keep
from drinking during lunch hours. God, the mints I used to suck

on to try to hide it when I went back to work! I didn't fool anybody. Kept getting fired. Finally joined my mother on welfare."

You know from your own experience that the decision to stop drinking or drugging is in some ways a mysterious one. Few recovering addicts and alcoholics can say exactly why they realized that they wanted to stop and get help to stay stopped. Michael is baffled by his own personal moment of truth. All he can do is describe the externals. "I was coming back from the liquor store on a typical Monday, the day my mother and I stocked up, after having drunk everything in the house over the weekend. I rounded the corner back to our building and there, right at my feet, was a pigeon. It was dying. There was something so terribly pathetic about it. I mean, most pigeons scatter out of your way when you walk toward them. But it was like this pigeon had just given up. Its eyes were still open, but its head had nestled down into the feathers. One wing, maybe broken, drooped down on the side.

"I can't describe what I felt. I wanted, first of all, to save it. Where was there a vet nearby, I wondered? Could I pick it up, or would I get some terrible disease from it? It fluttered its wing limply and cocked its head up at me, a tiny spark of fear in its eye. It was like it knew it was dying, and it was afraid. What could I do? God, I've never even noticed pigeons before. I'm not a big animal person or anything. But my heart went out to this little creature, dying there on the street, nobody but me caring about it. I—well, I guess I just lost it. I started to cry, sob. I had to lean against a lamppost while I poured out tears. I was crying for the pigeon, for all the things and creatures nobody cared about, for my dead father, for my dying mother—because yes, I knew at that moment, she was dying too, dying from booze just like my father had—and I cried for myself. Because I was dying as well."

Michael made a decision in that moment that changed his life. It wasn't so much that he wanted to stop drinking. He just wanted to stop *dying*. "It was the fact that I wanted to *live* that floored me," he said. "I'd gotten a glimpse, thanks to this dying bird, of what I was doing to myself. And I just didn't want to do it anymore."

Michael dropped the liquor he'd just bought into a trash can. "It was easy, all of a sudden. I had no qualms about it. God—that was a change, right there!" He trudged over to his church. He knew that AA meetings were held there, even if he didn't know when. "I sat in the basement room where I knew the meetings were held and just waited for the next one. Sat there for two and a half hours. I didn't mind. All I knew was I was ready for help." Eventually people began to troop in for a meeting. Michael can still remember the relief he felt. He knew he was in the right place from the moment the meeting started. "These people wanted to live too. That's all I knew. I wanted to be around people who wanted to live. Drinking meant death to me. I'd had enough of it."

Unfortunately, Michael's mother, with whom he still lives, hasn't "had enough of it." She still drinks. "I'm taking things really slowly," Michael says. "I've got a sponsor. I found a good outpatient therapy group for recovering addicts and alcoholics through people I met at that first meeting. I'm trying to read the literature, get to as many meetings as possible. But I'm still on welfare. I know it's too early to try to go back to work. I just don't have the stamina for it yet—or the brains! I can't concentrate on anything. My sponsor tells me, 'Be gentle with yourself. Just give yourself time to get sober.' " Michael takes a deep breath and frowns. "But he doesn't live with my mother!"

So many recovering addicts and alcoholics face Michael's problem. A spouse, lover, parent, sibling, roommate—whomever it is you still live with—may still be "active." How do you deal with booze and drugs in the house when you're trying to stay off them? "The simple answer is to get out," Michael says. "But I haven't been able to do that. For one thing, I can't afford to! We can barely afford the cheap rent my mother and I are paying on the welfare we both get. I just couldn't get enough to live on my own." So Michael has had to take some admittedly stopgap measures. Most of them have to do with organizing his day so that he's out of the house when he knows his mother is drinking—out doing things for himself that he knows will help him or will take up his time safely and enjoyably, not just out roaming around. "Not that I didn't do a lot of plain roaming around my first month," he says. "I couldn't make myself to go to meeting after meeting after meeting; after a while I felt I was overdosing on AA. But, slowly, I've found a place to do volunteer work, in a nursing home, where I just sit with old people, sometimes playing cards, sometimes just talking, sometimes just holding their hands. I'll save up sometimes to go to a movie. I'll do service at meetings. My sponsor suggested that I work up a daily calendar, filling in meetings first, then trying to come up with stuff at other times of the day that I'll like doing.

"It's hard. Sometimes I feel like it's so—I don't know— *contrived*. And I got so angry with my mother! The injustice of not feeling I can spend time in my own home really gets to me. But I try to remember she's an alcoholic. And I know from my own experience what that means. She's not going to stop until she wants to stop. And the hard truth is, that may be never."

Michael is working toward getting out of the apartment. He plans, tentatively, at the end of his first year of sobriety, to explore a preparatory program for recovering alcoholics reentering the work force. "First things first, I keep telling myself. I'm still so new, so raw in all this. I want to give myself as much time as I need. But eventually I'll get a job, and be able to afford someplace else. In the meantime, I've got to make the best of it. All I really know right now is that I don't want to drink. Even if my mother does."

People, places, and things almost always need to be looked at and changed in sobriety; few of us, in our "active" days, lived in a mentally, emotionally, and spiritually healthy environment, or surrounded ourselves with supportive and healthy people. Sometimes families can be called upon for support, and it's wonderful when that happens. Abby, a young woman in a small Ohio town who's been off drugs and alcohol for six months, beams with gratitude when she talks about what a support her parents have been to her, going to Al-Anon to understand the impact of this disease better, working in tandem with her therapist to help provide assistance that's both loving and effective. But, according to available evidence, Abby's experience is not common. All too often we've alienated those closest to us throughout our days, months, and years of drinking and drugging; by the time we enter recovery we may have no one around us, in or out of the family, to offer support. Or, just as commonly, the people in our families are as alcoholic or addicted as we are; we may come from a long, continuing history of abuse and pain (for whatever confluence of "nature and nurture" reasons, addiction does tend to run in families).

Extracting ourselves from people-meshes isn't always easy. But there do always seem to be better and worse next moves. Michael again: "Even when my mother's drunk, I've learned I don't have to let it drag me down. For one thing, I can go to Al-Anon, something a lot of my recovering friends with alcoholic family members are doing. But the main thing is, there's always someone I can call, someplace I can go, something I can do that will move me a little closer to recovery, even in the midst of my mother's alcoholic hell. And I live in the hope—the prayerful hope—that maybe something I'm doing in my own life might be an example to her. Maybe she'll stop someday too."

It's a truism that attempting to "Twelve Step" a family member (encourage him or her to get sober) is risky. Our relationships with family members are so charged that we rarely can muster enough objective distance to be truly helpful. Michael's sponsor tells him to pull back on the reins whenever he feels the urge to "coerce" his mother into "changing her ways." "I'm learning those are times I've got to do something for *myself*, not for her," Michael says. Which means he's got to return, once again, to his calendar, restructuring his time in sobriety so that he's as sure as he can be that he's getting what he needs to stay sober, to stay alive.

The main message I've gotten from recovering people is that we need to be especially gentle and permissive with ourselves as we begin to work out the details of our new sober lives. But a great worry for a lot of recovering people is that the lives they're "working out" will end up being boring. "What could ever replace the excitement of getting high, and having sex, and eating a lot, and all those other things I did when I was active?" one recovering addict asks. Another friend, in response to the mashed potatoes and sitcom story at the beginning of this chapter, groaned. "I don't want to be *ordinary*. God, is that what you're saying recovery is all about? Being ordinary?"

Strangely, giving yourself permission to try out a few "normal" or "ordinary" ways of spending time (like going home after work, cooking yourself nutritious meals, showing up on time for appointments, and all the rest of the stuff you may never have done or wanted to do before) rarely ends up being boring. In fact, it can have some surprising dividends. To begin with, there's the not inconsiderable feeling of relief. Trying on the idea that you're "one among many," that you don't have to spend every moment in an intense state of competition striving to be the best (or worst), can allow a wonderful feeling of serenity. But something more interesting seems to happen too. As you give yourself permission to slow down, to do simple positive things in your life, you often find that you're allowing a whole new self to emerge, one that's a hell of a lot more interesting and unusual than the stuck-in-a-rut drunk or drug addict you were before sobriety.

Recovering people teach me that the task of recovery isn't to level us into a state of numbed conformity. It's to clear the channels in our lives so that we have a chance of discovering what it is we really *do* want to do—who each of us really is. You may already have heard in Twelve Step meetings that recovery can bring you a life "beyond your wildest dreams." You may then have cynically thought to yourself, "Yeah, right. I'll be the best little homemaker on the block. Make a mean macaroni and cheese someday." However, as you'll eventually see in people who keep at this process, and in your own life if you keep at it, there are no limits to what's possible in sobriety. Don't take my or anyone else's word for that. Abundant evidence indicates you'll find it out for yourself if you hang in long enough, if you allow yourself to "wait," as Twelve Step people say, "for the miracle."

Developing patience as we learn to restructure our time does seem to be crucial to maintaining sobriety. Trial and error mark every new attempt to fill our days with something other than alcohol and drugs; progress is almost always stumbling. A sense of humor is a boon, and, again, Twelve Step meetings can help us out a lot in this regard. They're often hilarious. Why? Because our progress in sobriety, halting and uncertain as it usually is, seems to make us acutely sensitive to absurdity—the absurdity of old assumptions suddenly brought to new light, as we start to see the strange ways in which we've determinedly ignored some pretty obvious stuff about ourselves. "Alcoholics aren't very good at dealing with three things," says one recovering alcoholic friend. "Success, failure, and the obvious."

Michael sums all of this up, for himself and for many of the rest of us: "The key idea is permission. I'm *allowed* to make an ass of myself, to laugh at and let up on myself. Nobody's perfect, least of all someone trying to get sober for the first time in his life. It's okay to trip up sometimes. And what could happen to me that would be more terrible than living my old drunken life, or even more than that, how it felt? I've already *been* through the worst." The more Michael shares what he's going through with others, and the more we share what we're going through with other recovering people, the more fully we all seem to participate in the miracle of "getting better."

Twelve Step programs offer so much help, letting us see at every turn that we don't ever have to face sobriety alone. We'll try to make this as clear as we can in the next section of this book, by giving you a sense of what it's like to take this "sobriety act" on the road—how even newfound sobriety has prepared so many men and women to deal with their jobs, lovers, spouses, families, and friends in wholly new and much more effective ways.

This "out on the road" message is especially crucial. A fairly common complaint I've heard from newly sober people in Twelve Step programs runs, "Sure, this is all great as long as I'm spending time at meetings with other people. But what happens when I walk out the door?" "Walking out the door" may mean facing your mother, your lover, your spouse, your kids, your boss, your former drug dealer, the welfare office, or the next office cocktail party. It may mean facing sex, friendship, the corner deli (where the beer may still look *very* good), or the prospect of telling your old drinking or drugging buddies that you no longer indulge. It may mean dealing with anger, resentment, and frustration even greater than you've encountered in the average AA or NA business meeting—which, if you've been to one, you'll realize is saying something!

Let's listen to a few people who have taken their first steps out into the "Real World" and survived. Even thrived. And all without picking up a drink or a drug.

five

Love, Family, Work (and Your Cat):
"Real Life" in Sobriety

A common rude awakening to many newly recovering people coming off live-in rehabs is that the world does not care about them the way their rehabs did. They may know and even anticipate this intellectually, but the *experience* of passing enticing displays in liquor stores, come-ons from streetwalkers, good-Joe invitations to have a beer, knowing winks from drug dealers, not to mention the greedy, even cruel attitudes of so many people who have decidedly *not* made the decision to turn their lives and wills over to a Power greater than themselves—all of this can throw you, to say the least. We inevitably discover not only that life is not a rehab, but that few people outside of "the program" especially care whether or not we pick up a drink or drug. In fact, more than a few would be very happy to get us drinking and drugging again.

A lot of people react badly to this reality. Feeling in some vague but painful way betrayed by the world, unable to deal with the sudden onslaught of "real life," they do exactly what they'd told themselves they'd never do again: pick up alcohol or drugs and resume the process of killing themselves. This rude awakening isn't limited to people newly loosed from rehabs, of course. It can happen to anyone who ventures out the door of a Twelve Step meeting into the uncaring commerce of the rest of the world.

How do you navigate these shoals?

First, perhaps, by attempting to map out what they are. Freud gives us a clue. He says we're happy if we're happy in two areas of life: love and work. Love and work are certainly two burning topics for recovering addicts and alcoholics, judging from my evidence. And we seem to worry about a third category nearly as much: family—or, more precisely, dealing with the effects of family, past and present. In fact, according to what I've learned from scores of recovering addicts and alcoholics across the country, and especially from people in their first year of sobriety, family, love, and work constitute possibly the three largest "mountains" to be climbed in sober life.

Let's start with the "love" part. It's often the most overbearing arena we enter as we first get sober. Sex, love, and intimacy can plague us pretty urgently in our first days, weeks, and months of sobriety. Dealing with relationships, or the lack of them, usually requires some real adjustments in attitude and behavior. Sometimes the craving for intimate contact in sobriety can become so acute you think you'll go mad. At other times the prospect of having to deal with anyone on an intimate level fills you with the worst kind of dread. "Damned if you do, damned if you don't" characterizes this whole area for many of us. But, as with every other aspect of recovery we've looked at so far, the particulars of our experience vary a great deal. Let's look at a few of those "intimate" particulars, and, more important, how a number of newly sober people are managing to deal with them in productive ways.

Love, Sex, and Intimacy
—or the Lack of It—
in Early Sobriety

You go home and there he or she is or there he or she isn't. Sometimes you're glad there's someone to go home to—or that there isn't. Just as often you're devastated.

One reassuring realization that comes to many newly recovering people as they go to more and more meetings is that people can be happy or unhappy whether they're alone *or* in a relationship. This reminds us of, and reinforces, a central awareness of sobriety: What happens outside us isn't as important as what happens inside. You may think "if only" you had the perfect lover you'd be happy—but go to enough meetings and listen to people who are in love relationships and you'll soon hear a different "if only": "If only I weren't trapped in this relationship!" It eventually dawns on us that the "perfect lover" may not be what will "fix" us after all. Working on the Steps, especially, seems to teach us on deeper and deeper levels that *we* are accountable for our lives; blaming our dissatisfaction on what (or who) we don't have is almost always wrongheaded. Satisfaction, we learn, can't come from acquiring things or people; it seems to be the result of a different "inside job." And nowhere does this message seem more urgently applicable than in the zone of love, sex, and intimacy.

Manny provides a vivid illustration.

Manny is a runner: That's what you think when you look at him. He is lean to the point of emaciation. There's a hunted look in his eyes, only barely softened by his first six and a half months of sobriety. With his James Dean look, Manny is also immensely attractive. Nearing forty, he could pass for twenty-five. He's the sort of "wounded animal" that has appealed to all too many people certain they could take care of him. He knows he's got this power, and when he drank, he made abundant use of it.

"I wouldn't be able to tell you how many women I've been involved with. I lost count ten or fifteen years ago," Manny explains, not bragging but rather stating a simple fact. "I've been to shrinks. I've got all sorts of good reasons for why I'm not good at intimacy. Getting the shit beat out of me by my alcoholic father was part of it. Feeling I had to take care of my mother from about the age of six—that's another part. Having four older brothers who resented me for being the baby and gave me hell when I was growing up . . . I'm not complaining; that's just how it was. My self-esteem has always been about zero. Only thing I could ever do well is run. Won a scholarship in track to the state university. Was a big shot there. That's also where I found out I could drink as much as my father ever could. And where I found that certain women seemed to find me attractive. Running, booze, and a succession of intense sexual affairs, one after the other. Wasn't a bad life, really. Except . . ." Smiling isn't something Manny does often, but he manages an ironic grin now. "It was never enough. Not enough danger. That's when I started breaking into houses, my last year of college. Not so much for the stuff I could steal, but for the thrill of it. That's also when I stopped having 'relationships'—which were wearing me down, what with women wanting commitment and me to fall in love and all that—and started going out with whores. Irish bars where you drank seriously, women you paid for serious sex, and serious fun like risking your life hanging from a three-story ledge of a building you'd just robbed: that was more like it. That was closer to— I don't know. Death, maybe."

Manny got caught in every sense about a year ago. A patrol car happened to be passing just as he leapt out of an apartment building window after a robbery: The cop was quick. Manny was handcuffed and on his way to jail. A routine prejail physical, complete with blood tests, indicated that Manny had the HIV virus, which he imagines he got from prostitutes. He got out of jail in five months; it was his first arrest, and his sullen, resigned obedience counted as "good behavior." He felt, when he got out, "death-bound. I just waited around for the first signs of full-blown AIDS to hit," he said. "It was somehow satisfying. Especially as I started to drink again. It was funny, I didn't really miss drinking in jail. In fact, I liked the fact that jail just squeezed the freedom out of me. Turned me into a gray nobody. It was like, bad as it was, somebody at least was taking care of me. Now that

I was out, I decided to drink and wait to die. What else was in the cards for me? I was luckier than my dad. I had more than alcohol killing me. I thought I also had, or was going to have, AIDS. Death was a real sure bet in my case."

Manny was on welfare in an SRO hotel drinking nonstop pints of cheap wine when something happened to change the pattern of his life. He inherited a cat. "An old lady died down the hall. Fairly typical case: The rest of us tenants smelled her—it was August—a good number of days after she'd keeled over from a heart attack. They took her body away. They also let out a very hungry little cat from her room. For some reason the cat made a beeline for my door. Nobody seemed to care or notice, so I let the thing in. Started feeding it. Call her Rosie—that was the old lady's name. A little legacy, anyway, from a woman the rest of the world had sure as hell forgotten."

The cat was the first responsibility Manny could ever recall wanting to have. He says, in fact, that it was the cat that gave him the idea of getting sober. "I'd pass out sometimes, and the cat wouldn't get fed. Then I'd come to and see the thing, hungry, alone, nobody to take care of it but me. It started to bug me. The thing wasn't asking anything of me but to give it food, clean its shit up, simple stuff like that. Wasn't like a human being who wanted to have psychological conversations with me. I started feeling bad about it. I began to realize something strange: I actually loved something. I loved the cat. It seemed to love me, maybe that's part of why I loved it. But for some reason it made me, for the first time, have second thoughts about wanting to die so soon."

Manny knew about AA; he'd even been to some meetings as the result of this or that long-ago ultimatum from one of his dozens of women. He started going to meetings again. "I didn't go for me," he says, allowing another rare smile to transform his face. "I went for my cat." But Manny's attitudes have changed, slowly, over the past six or seven months. "All I did at first was sit at the back of the room in the smoking section of meetings and smoke. Felt a little like school. You know, people jabbering at you while you just sat there in the back drifting away. But something started getting through to me. I don't know what exactly. It's like something unconscious in me, something down way deep inside, was getting 'fed,' just like my cat got fed when I took care of it. It almost didn't matter what anyone was talking about in meetings. Just the fact that they were *there*, that people were sticking together, trying to keep from drinking, trying to get through life. I don't know, it started to move me. So when people began to notice me, ask me out to coffee and stuff, I actually went. I wanted more of whatever it was I was getting at meetings."

It was a feeling of making contact, but different from the intense "orgasmic" experiences with women Manny had known before as the only satisfying way of connecting with people. "Intimacy to me always meant sex. Why else would I be with a woman except to have sex with her? But here I was, listening to women and men, not getting freaked out, just being—normal. It was confusing." Manny says the old cravings, which he realized fueled his compulsive drinking and whoring in the past, started to reawaken. "I started walking down the old streets, all my ladies waiting for me. Finally thought I'd compromise with a peep show in the combat zone of the city. Went in and—well, 'took care of myself,' watching this drugged-out naked lady lit up by blue light." It had its "excitements," Manny said, but his simple physical orgasm didn't take away a deeper craving. "I realized then I wasn't just out for that. I was out for something else, something more important. In fact, it was funny. The only satisfying thing I could imagine doing right then was to go home quick and spend time with my cat."

This gave Manny some insight. The only unconditional love he'd ever known, or ever expressed, was for his cat. "Something went on between me and that animal that was more important than any other feeling I'd ever had about another creature on the planet," Manny said. "I got home, took the cat in my arms, and I cried. The cat squirmed a little, then licked my face and purred. I felt what I guess I'd been waiting my whole life to feel. Some creature accepted me, totally, just as I was, and loved me, no questions asked. I guess that's what was pulling me to AA too. I know it was. I could go someplace and be loved. That's what was helping me to stay sober, to want to live. That pull of unconditional acceptance and understanding. I even see my HIV status differently. Not sure why. But it doesn't seem like a death sentence, anymore than life is a death sentence. Nobody gets off the planet alive, after all. But, I don't know, my cat and AA teach me that I can live more satisfyingly in the moment than I ever thought I could. The key is some kind of real self-acceptance. And some ability to accept the love that, it turns out, is all around me." Manny shakes his head. "Is this me talking?" Another of his smiles, which are starting to come far less rarely. His cat nudges his hand, demanding to be petted. "Yeah. Blame my cat, but it's me talking. . . ."

The absence of a sexual relationship was not Manny's problem as much as he thought it was. The deeper problem was connecting to some strong sense of himself as acceptable, lovable, "enough." Sometimes when we're able to look beneath our own urgent cravings we too find surprises: We often discover we're not after what we thought we were. Certainly sexual cravings commonly hide a host of other, deeper desires—longings that may turn out to be more for unconditional love than unceasing sex.

Not that we don't experience some genuine sexual frustrations sometimes. Marcia, a woman in her mid-fifties who is just nearing the end of her first year in AA and NA, "rediscovered the power of sex," as she puts it, after a couple of years of self-imposed celibacy. "I'd just written off sex in my life," Marcia says. "I was too old, not attractive enough anymore. The world, and especially the sexual world, was structured to work for people twenty, thirty years younger than I. But then I got together with an ex-husband and we decided 'for old time's sake' to go to bed together again. It was incredible. I honestly didn't know what it would be like now that I wasn't drunk. It was—amazing. I actually *felt* what was happening to me. It was real in a way I'd never experienced anything before." Now, she says, she feels like a tap has been turned on she doesn't know how to turn off. "Sometimes I think I'll go crazy. I'm on the verge of hiring a gigolo! I realize that, given half a chance, I could easily turn this into a repeat of when I drank and took pills: I couldn't get enough sex, I don't think!" She takes a deep breath. "My sponsor says as long as I don't pull off someone's pants in the middle of the street, as long as I keep acting in a way that won't get me into trouble, I'm taking care of myself in some *basic,* safe way. But she also suggests that I look a little harder at the frustrations, the triggers, that particularly get my sexual hungers going. To see what else might be going on."

It's not that Marcia doesn't have the perfect right to explore how she might, eventually, want to pursue fulfillment in her life, including sexual fulfillment. But she's realizing now that, at least in her early sobriety, she has to be careful about her behavior in this very charged, very powerful area. "It's enough, still, to stay sober one day at a time. I'm now opting for a bit more celibacy, I think—at least for a while, as I continue to get more comfortable being who I am as a newly sober woman. How all this will eventually work out—well, thank God for the Third Step, the idea of turning all this over to God. Let *Him* do something with all this! *I* can't."

Just as commonly, of course, newly sober people find that the idea of sex without getting high is distasteful, if not terrifying. A major function of drugs and alcohol for many of us was precisely to rid us of sexual inhibitions. Alcohol and drugs can be terrific "superego solvents" that enable us to let loose, fantasize wildly, objectify our partners into some close approximation of our sexual ideal. Now that we're not getting high, and we see our partners more as real human beings than as hallucinated sex objects, sex can be an unnerving shock.

Luckily, we've got a very strong program waiting for us that tells us to "keep it simple." We don't have to solve all of our problems with love, sex, and intimacy right now. We are tremendous successes simply because we've managed to get through one more day sober.

The wisdom of "don't make any major changes in your first year" becomes palpably evident in the area of relationships. Jack, a thirty-five-year-old man who's been with his lover, Bill, for six years—a little more than five of those years drunk—thanks God for Al-Anon too. "Bill couldn't understand why I was so withdrawn around him. Now that I wasn't drinking and drugging anymore, why hadn't I turned into the perfect, good-guy, sensitive, normal lover he was sure I'd be? But in Al-Anon he's learning what a shock to an addict's system early sobriety can be. That it's all I can do, sometimes, to get up out of bed, take care of myself, get through the day, go to meetings, eat a normal meal, go to sleep. I can't have a 'relationship' right now. I need some space simply to *be*. A lot of stuff between us has to go on the shelf. We're getting better now at signaling 'Time Out' when we hit yet another stalemate. Like why I don't want to have sex right now. Like why I can't stay up past nine o'clock at night. God knows how all this stuff will work out in the future. I can't worry about that now. I'm trying too hard to get through the basics—to deal with day-to-day life—sober."

Another common problem for people who are in relationships, sober, that they got into when they were drinking and drugging, is having to face the fact that their relationship may not be able to survive sobriety. Angelique, a Haitian immigrant who moved to Florida with her husband ten years ago, says that she comes from a background in which "the wife belongs to the husband, pure and simple. But now that I'm sober, now that I'm finding friends outside the family who are sober too, I'm starting to become a whole new woman. And I don't like the life I had when I drank. I was my husband's servant. He is confused. What happened to his live-in cook, maid, lover? Why do I question his authority? Something will have to change; something already has changed. I don't know if we can work this out. I can't really blame him: He married a woman, now he finds he's married to another. We'll see what we can do, but we may not be able to stay together."

What seems to emerge in each of the stories about intimacy that newly sober people have shared with me is the necessity of calling "Time Out," as Jack says he does with Bill when they get to a "stalemate." The complexities of having a relationship (or not having a relationship) are forbidding and seemingly inevitable; they can easily threaten to overwhelm us. It can be so tempting to get to the "Oh, screw it!" end of our tethers and decide "It's just not worth it—I might as well drink and drug." But remember what we've already explored about the onslaught of feelings in early sobriety. They pass. First-year recoverers seem especially to profit from remembering that bit of wisdom as it applies to love, sex, and intimacy. As urgent as your feelings of self-pity, anger, jealousy, loneliness, or sexual and romantic craving can be, they are only temporary. "Hanging on to let go" can allow you to discover that your powerful emotions and cravings are usually telling you something deeper and more interesting than they at first appeared to be. To find this out, you have only to let them happen, *and pass*—which they will.

The intensity of our cravings related to love sometimes doesn't hold a candle to the degree of exasperation we can feel about our family, especially in early sobriety. Let's take a closer look at mommy, daddy, and homicidal urges, among other family-related topics.

Family

Not all families are "dysfunctional." But in sobriety, we do seem to become acutely aware of the degree to which our families have affected, all too often negatively, our pasts and presents. So many of the "if onlys" I've heard from newly recovering addicts and alcoholics run along the lines of "If only my family hadn't been a bunch of drunks"; "If only my father hadn't left home"; "If only my mother had given me love"; "If only they'd given me the attention they gave my sister"; "If only they hadn't beaten me"; "If only I hadn't been sexually abused. . . ." None of these "if onlys" is trivial; in fact, all need to be looked at carefully, a process for which the Twelve Steps offer guidance. But the ongoing, festering resentment that these "if onlys" encourage—however justified the resentment may be—can become a formidable obstacle to achieving a happy life in sobriety. And what we resent isn't, of course, only memories of the past. Problems with family often plague us quite vividly in sobriety today. Remember Michael, who still lives with his alcoholic mother? He, like many of the rest of us, has had to continue to deal with some difficult and immediate family problems from day one of sobriety.

It is possible, of course, to get wonderful support from your family as you first get sober; you may recall our brief mention of Abby in Ohio whose family actively explored what addiction was all about, went to Al-Anon, and have collectively become a mainstay of help and nurturing for Abby. But sometimes, even when family intentions appear to be supportive, things can backfire, or at least get difficult.

Witness the problems Nan has had with her own mother and father, now that she's ten months sober.

At twenty-eight, Nan feels she's spent her whole life trying to be what others wanted her to be, striving to make her appearance and the trappings of her life "acceptable." She hasn't had Susan's burden of being black in an all-white town and feeling she had to set an example for her entire race; her antecedents were about as WASP as anyone's could be. In fact, as Nan sees it, that was part of the problem. "My forebears virtually came over on the *Mayflower*—well, one branch came over to Virginia, but at about the same respectable seventeenth-century time. One thing drummed into me from the moment I was born was that I was special. Some kind of aristocracy. Not that we ever had all that much money. We had what my father and grandfather said was much more important than money, and much less vulgar. We had 'standing.' I was never sure what that meant, exactly. I only knew I was supposed to live up to it, with every breath or action I took." Nan groans a little, and shakes her shoulders, as if to shed this heavy family mantle.

Nan says she rarely drank more than four glasses of wine a night, and it never occurred to her, just as it had never occurred to Susan, that she was an alcoholic. But in other ways she knew she was compulsive. "I was a madwoman with credit cards. It was like these little pieces of plastic would pull me out of the house—they *had* to be used." Nan was aware that her debt-inducing shopping expeditions were tied to anxiety. She knew anxiety had a lot to do with her "food problem" too. "I never quite got bulimic, but the thought wasn't at all unappealing. I'd binge and then fast for days, then binge again and fast. I popped Dexatrim like candy. I was a mess. Somehow I kept my weight down, but it was nuts. I was miserable, grasping for anything I could to get outside myself. I had this whole system of reward and punishment with food—from a quart of ice cream to days of nothing but hot water and lemon. And, of course, wine. I remember once running out on Saturday, late, and realizing I'd have nothing to drink the next day, Sunday. I actually went into a cold sweat, a real panic. I couldn't imagine not having that security—the security of knowing I could 'relax' the following night with a few drinks. I just couldn't imagine going on without every jagged piece of my life crammed into place. I see my life back then as this unwieldy patchwork thing, with all sorts of requirements—stuff that had to be held up and balanced and maintained with exhausting vigilance. I'd pretty much given up on the idea of ever finding a man. I suppose I'm attractive enough, but I couldn't imagine anyone putting up with someone as neurotic as me! And whenever any man—or any person, really—had ever tried to show me affection or love in the past, something in me didn't register it. I just shut down. Maybe I couldn't believe anyone *could* love me. I don't know. Shopping, food, and drinking were my only vents. And, God, my *work!* How could I not mention *that?* I'm a receptionist at a classy law firm and I always prided myself on my efficiency, and how everyone liked me—it was so important that everyone like me! I couldn't take the least bit of criticism, and I guess it showed. After a while nobody did criticize me; only later did I find out that they were all afraid I'd have a breakdown if they ever tried! I found the perfect people to work for: They were scared of me and I was scared of them."

The pressure of Nan's life built and built until, one evening when she got home from a particularly tense day at work and realized she didn't have enough wine in the house to get her through the night, she "broke." "I just started sobbing. I sat there at the kitchen table, my head in my arms, and sobbed. I thought I'd never stop. It was some horrible, relentless torrent of stuff— like something was getting pulled out of my gut, and it would never stop coming out, it would always hurt." Nan called in sick the next day, and the next. A week went by and still she was unable to go to work. "I bundled myself up in bed—I'd only gone out to get a case of cheap Italian dry wine—and did nothing but sip and tremble and pass out, then sip and tremble and pass out again. I still didn't think of myself as alcoholic. I knew that I was going through a bad time, and this was just the only 'medicine' I had. But *drinking* wasn't the problem. The problem was how neurotic I was!"

Finally, when Nan realized she felt trapped in a way she'd

never felt before, she found the courage, somehow, to call a hot-line for people who thought they had a drinking problem. "I could just as easily have called the suicide hotline. Or a hotline for depression. Or for eating disorders. Or anything! But drinking was what I was doing, and it was all I could think of looking up; I'd seen some ad for this hotline in a bus. I called Directory Assistance for the number, and I used it."

Nan eventually got taken to her first AA meeting by someone she met through the hotline organization she phoned. The sense of connecting we've already seen in so many people in this book began to take hold for her, and she started to get—and *feel*—sober. "Giving up my wine wasn't as hard as I thought it would be," Nan says. "Maybe it was just so wonderful to feel there were people I could *talk* to that it distracted me from missing it. But I still wasn't sure I was one of 'them.' God, the stories some of them told, the horrible degrading bottoms they hit! I hadn't experienced anything like that. All I know, though, is that there was *some-thing* healing going on, and I felt it, and wanted more of it."

In fact, Nan's new positive feelings built up to such a degree that she decided she wanted to tell her family what she was do-ing. "I'd always had these ritual calls from my mother every week: 'How are you dear?' 'Fine.' 'How's the job?' 'Fine.' 'Meet any interesting people?' By this my mother meant had I met a marriageable WASP lawyer yet. 'No, Mother, not really.' 'Well, keep at it, darling!' and then the litany of church and community and family news. That was about it between me and my folks. To Dad the phone was a self-indulgence; he believed it was something you should only use for emergencies, like to commu-nicate somebody's sudden tragic death. So I almost never talked to him." Nan smiles a little, then her brow creases. "I don't know why I wanted to share this 'recovery' business with them, really," she continues. "It's not like we ever shared anything be-neath the surface of our lives before. But maybe—well, maybe that was it. We *hadn't* shared anything important. I was sorry for that. I wanted them to know who I was—that I was in pain, and getting better. I wanted to break the *Ordinary People* script our lives always seemed to have been." Nan arranged a weekend trip home. "Is anything wrong?" she says her parents asked. She explained that she just wanted to see them, spend some time with them.

"That Friday morning I almost canceled. What was I doing? How on earth was I going to tell them all I wanted to say? That I thought I was an alcoholic? That I had just gone through one of the most horrible bouts of anxiety imaginable and had come close to killing myself? How could I say these things to people whose lives were filled with church suppers, family history, and 'standing'? Maybe there was something, I don't know, really rebellious in me. Maybe I wanted to throw a few grenades—wake them up to my pain. Let them see their daughter as something *dangerous*—or at least three-dimensional! I don't know."

Whatever Nan might have hoped for during that weekend, it didn't happen. "It was an unmitigated disaster," she said. "Not, strangely, that they weren't supportive. In their way, they were perfectly supportive. In fact, when I first told my mother I was going to AA, she smiled sweetly and patted my hand. 'Oh, isn't that some nice support group, where people get together and talk about things?' She had some vague idea it was, I don't know, a kind of Junior League discussion group where you talked about lofty subjects, reverently. I explained to her that AA stood for 'Alcoholics Anonymous.' And *then*—" Nan's eyes blaze with fury. "Then you'll never guess what happened. My father and my mother *laughed!*"

Nan's father was the first to speak. "Oh, Nan, this is just like that time you were thirteen and decided you'd become a nun! Remember that, honey? You drew all sorts of pictures of black robes and chanted Hail Marys, poor darling. The things you won't come up with!" Nan says her mother managed to quiet her father's glee, now patting *his* hand ("patting hands is big with my mother"), and said, "I'm sorry, dear, *please* forgive your father—but surely this is for some sort of class you're taking, isn't it? Weren't you going take some evening classes in psychology a while back?"

Then, Nan says, she "lost it." Starting in what she remembers as a "lethally, level, quiet voice," ending in a torrent of tears nearly as bad as the sobbing she'd done right before joining AA, she ripped into her story, her feelings of isolation, her belief that she'd never been understood or really loved by her parents, the fact that she was a food-abusing, in-debt-up-to-her-ears, neurotic alcoholic. She told her story, every bit of it, with every bit of venom she'd stored up her whole life against her parents.

"My parents looked shell-shocked," Nan says. "And for a moment, I thought I'd gotten through to them. They said they were sorry I was in so much pain. They even said they were glad I was seeking help—if AA was some kind of therapy, well, they thought that was very nice. But then my mother took over; she got her usual 'knowing' look, the one where she feels she and only she has the answer, and it would behoove us all to take notes, thank you very much. 'Now, Nan,' she said. 'I've been worried about you for a long time. You're nearly thirty years old, and *of course* you're frustrated. Why, if I had waited until I was thirty before finding a good man and starting a family, I might have made up problems like these too! Now that you've stopped all this foolish behavior—drinking a little too much and the rest of it—now that you're all better, why not put a little Yankee effort into meeting a good man and settling down? You know, Grace next door was telling me about this marvelous Princeton Club dance next month . . ."

Nan said she felt like someone had pulled out a plug somewhere in her and let all the air out. "I felt steamrolled. Hopeless. My parents and I were on such different planets. And worse, I started to doubt my own sanity. *Was* I making up these problems? Loony as my mother was, did she have a point there?

I started to doubt everything I'd begun to trust in the program. Higher Power—what sort of nonsense was that? Surrender? Surrender what to whom? I'd never felt more depressed. I returned to my old quiet withdrawn self, let my mother go on and on. Life just flattened out for me. Completely flattened out. There was no such thing anymore as hope."

It's taken some time for Nan to recover from this sense of hopelessness. She's thankful, now, that she could come back from this devastating trip and make herself go to meetings—and, more important, to talk about her doubts, her feelings that nothing, not even AA, could help her. Recovery resumed as she listened to the "experience, strength, and hope" of other people who'd grappled with similar doubts and somehow moved beyond them. "I learned a lot about what really happened with my parents," Nan says. "First of all, that you can't explain recovery to anyone who isn't receptive to it. This may seem obvious, but I guess I was so happy with the new, growing, positive feelings I had that I wanted to evangelize—sort of preach the program to everyone else! I wanted other people to enjoy what I was enjoying. But I've noticed, not only with my parents but with friends of mine who aren't in the program, that people just don't get it. They still think that quitting drinking or drugging is some pure matter of willpower. That's even what my father said. He said, 'Of course you were able to give all the stuff up! You're my daughter, aren't you? Everyone in our family can do what they put their minds to!' There was no sense—no sense *at all*—that the process I'm undergoing, that anyone who is recovering undergoes, has to do with *surrender*. And that there's some kind of spiritual help going on. It isn't that old Protestant ethic of pulling yourself up by your own bootstraps. Sure, I need all the willpower I can get. But I know that's not at the root of why I'm recovering."

Now Nan isn't expecting her parents to come up with empathy or insight that experience has taught her they simply don't have. "It's like I've heard in the rooms," she says. "Don't go to a hardware store for oranges. Don't try to get from people what they're incapable of giving you." Nan is also learning to keep her impulses to "evangelize" at bay, sharing with other recovering people what she knows from experience nobody else can really understand. "I realize from listening to people whose sobriety I admire that they're attractive to me not because they're trying to cram anything down my throat, but because their *lives* have become examples. All they have to do to help me is be themselves."

Nan has discovered that sometimes you can improve your relationships with people, including your family, *just by being your sober self.* You don't have to sell anyone anything. Simply living by Twelve Step principles, continuing not to drink or drug, and going to meetings can set up an amazingly positive domino effect. People generally notice by themselves that you've changed. In my experience, and in that of recovering people I've talked to, recovery can even be contagious. Others become curious about what it is that's transformed you, that's calmed you down, given you a new, sometimes radiant sense of serenity.

Not that you can bank on this happening all the time. One recovering man with nine months of sobriety steeled himself to visit his highly "active" family who lived in the small town in South Carolina where he'd grown up. Jerry hadn't been home for three years, and with only nine months of sobriety, he was frightened by how he might react to what he called his "lunatic, drunken, drugged-out" family. Still, he wanted to try. He called ahead to arrange to be picked up by Twelve Step people and taken to meetings. And he took the train home in the hope of being able to survive a week.

He was back in three days. "I couldn't take it," Jerry says. "I simply wasn't ready for all that craziness. They kept expecting me to be the old me and kept reacting to me as if I were. That's what frightened me most of all. If I'd stayed there longer, I think I might have obliged them—just given up. 'You want me to be an asshole? Okay, you win. Pass me the booze and reefer.' It was just too early to go back home. I still need some distance."

The distance we sometimes discover we need to put between ourselves and people we love can be saddening. But, as recovering people make clear from hard experience, our sobriety has to come first. When we can't make families a part of our recovery—when, in fact, they get in the way of it—we may have to go another way. Of course, as we've suggested, you may find that the sober person you become as you go on in the program can effect some seemingly miraculous and positive changes in how your family reacts to you. As you become more reliable, more consistent emotionally, as others see that you're not going off the deep end on any regular basis, you may discover new capacities in yourself and your family for closeness and communion. So many family relationships get better as a simple result of one family member getting sober. But whether or not you experience that happy dividend, one thing seems clear: *Sobriety has to come first.* Remember the danger Michael faces, going home every day to his drunken mother. Every day is a lesson to him—the lesson that to survive he must (to borrow an Al-Anon phrase) "keep the focus on himself."

The highly charged feelings we can't seem to help bringing to lovers, spouses, and family can extend to another area of our lives: who we are and what we think, worry, and dream about in our work lives. As we first get sober, having a job or not having one can offer us some formidable emotional challenges. Let's quickly look at a few sides of this, to see how it's possible to deal with any side without resorting to old, self-destructive behaviors.

Work and Self-Worth

A recovering friend informed me recently of a scientific survey of animal behavior that determined that a certain kind of shrew (living—mostly sleeping—underground) devoted less than 1 percent of its time to "work," which meant, in its case, foraging for food. What a role model! Over 99 percent of your life spent not working? Sounded great to him.

It doesn't sound so great to recovering people at the other end of the spectrum—those who think of themselves as "workaholics." With the all-or-nothing attitudes common to many of us, the wild pendulum swings between extremes that seem to characterize our feelings about just about everything: We want either to be crammed full of activity or to be allowed to do nothing at all.

Work is a scary business for us. You'll remember the freelance editor Sharon, from the "Having Feelings" section, who discovered in early sobriety that she just couldn't concentrate on big projects when she got sober—that it was enough to learn to shop at a supermarket and wash her kitchen floor. Or Michael, living with his alcoholic mother, having to acknowledge that all he could do was stay sober one day at a time in his first year; work was just more than he could handle. Not everyone feels this way, of course. You've also met a number of men and women in this book who have been able to keep their jobs going at a fairly even keel. Phillip, our conscientious college librarian, somehow managed to remain "conscientious" during and after his drinking. Other people we've met couldn't understand how they ever had time to drink or drug back in their "active" days; their days are so full of work and meetings and relationships now, even in the first months of their sobriety.

Certainly there's a range of reactions in early sobriety to the prospect of work. But we all seem to slam into one universal truth about it: Work is how so many of us have defined our *worth*. Recovering addicts and alcoholics tend to get highly sensitive, frightened, and confused when the topic of work comes up in a Twelve Step meeting. Suddenly we may find ourselves talking longer than usual, as if out of the need to justify whatever we're doing, whether it's staying in a job we hate, being out of work and not being able to find a job, or staying on welfare. However, just as difficult is reconciling ourselves to *success*—as pressing a dilemma for many of us as dealing with the perceived lack of it. It's confusing territory.

Andy, a thirty-six-year-old carpenter who does construction work for various contractors, is a big, burly man. It's not easy for him to admit to problems about anything. He says he was brought up to believe that a man keeps everything to himself; any expression of emotion meant weakness. But, in sobriety, he's starting to open up. And he's able to admit to having a particularly tough time with work in sobriety. "Before I got sober and stopped doing drugs, about eight months ago, I felt like one of the guys. That's the truth. I mean, you didn't work with guys like I work with and not drink and smoke some dope. That was part of the territory. It was part of being a man, a guy who could 'take it.'" Now that he's not drinking or drugging, but still working with a lot of the same people, Andy feels a lot of pressure. "'What's the matter?' they yell at me, 'A beer gonna screw up your poor little tummy?' I can't get mad at them, really. They're a bunch of drunks; that's why I hung out with them. Who wants to be around guys who don't get high when all you wanna do is get high? I understand that. But it still hurts."

Andy is having to find new jobs—wean himself away from the old "comfortable" working arrangements he'd once known, arrangements that are proving to be far from comfortable now. "I'm even thinking of going to night school and, like, learning engineering or something. Get into a whole new line where I don't have to work with these guys," Andy says. "But, you know, working with these guys was my whole life. They were my only friends. I still haven't clicked like that with anyone in AA or NA. It's hard admitting this, but I'm lonely."

We've already encountered the phrase "people, places, and things." We don't generally realize until we stop drinking and drugging how destructive so many of the external circumstances of our lives were. And it can be hard to wean yourself off them, especially when they once gave you all the security you knew. Andy is learning that his feelings of loneliness won't kill him— but drinking and drugging will. He's also able at least to give lip service to the belief that his loneliness will lift, just as he's seen other feelings lift even in his first few months of sobriety. "All I gotta do is remember how low I got when I got wasted," he says, "to stop pitying myself too much when the guys get on my back. I guess I'll hang in there whatever it takes. And take some steps to replace my old life with something new. That's what AA and NA keep telling me I can do."

Because we often identify ourselves so completely with what we "do," work issues can be very potent—potent enough to threaten our sobriety. Andy might easily have given in to his cronies' taunts and gone back to drinking and drugging. A lot of other people, faced with the same kind of peer pressure, have done exactly that. But we cheat ourselves when we give in. On the principle we've been exploring throughout this book—that even uncomfortable feelings can end up being instructive—the pain and dissatisfaction that work-related issues can make us feel often lead to a new kind of clarity about who we are and what we want. Which can turn out to be something quite different than we once thought.

Marilyn illustrates this. She was a CEO in a major advertising company—"an industry that *runs* on drugs and alcohol," she says—when she suddenly decided to give up her cocaine habit. "I knew it was screwing up my life, making me paranoid. 'Recovery' was suddenly becoming chic too. All the magazines were running articles about this or that celebrity who'd 'seen the light.' I moved in a very trendy crowd, so I decided I'd quit too. I started going to some Twelve Step meetings, and they did help. I even took some phone numbers, and called, late at night, when I felt like climbing the walls from wanting to do coke. But what

I didn't do was make any attempt to change my high-pressured work life. That was off-limits. That was something I felt had no matter what happened to me."

Ever self-disciplined, she didn't skip a beat the day after stopping her cocaine use. She kept all her appointments, drove herself as hard as ever. "My work life was always completely compartmentalized away from my private life," she says. "I forced myself to get to work, in the old days, even when I had my worst cocaine paranoid attacks. I forced myself to be charming, efficient, persuasive—whatever I had to be. What I really was successful at was acting! I would have died before admitting I had a drug problem. I would have died before admitting I was *human*, for that matter!"

Marilyn began to question her approach to work when she finally got a sponsor. "I'd booked a lunch date with my new sponsor, June, at some peculiar, compulsive-sounding time. Like, okay, we can meet at 12:35 two blocks away from my office as long as I can get back by 1:12 so that I can make the overseas calls I've got to make before 2:15 . . . that sort of thing. June was quiet; she just said okay. But when I met her, all she seemed interested in was what I did at work, what it meant to me, if I'd ever thought of slowing down and giving myself a little time to 'recover.' I felt annoyed. Why was she barging into my work life? I expressed my annoyance to her, asking her to keep out of what I felt was clearly not her business—literally and figuratively! She paused for a moment and asked me, 'So recovery is something you only do when you're out of the office?'"

Marilyn felt stopped in her tracks. "I began, at that moment, to question what exactly it was I wanted from recovery. What the work even meant to me." She sighs, and continues. "Suddenly what happened at the office seemed different to me. I began, slowly, to realize that I had never ever taken the time to ask myself a crucial question: *Is this really what I want to do?* I guess, until that time, I'd always thought a question like that was self-indulgent. All these old voices from my past rumbled in: 'Stop thinking of yourself!' 'Just do what I tell you!' 'You don't know what's best for you!' 'Yours is not to reason why! . . .' Work, for me, had become a kind of terrible prison, something I thought I had to be trapped in. I never realized that it was part of life. That I didn't turn off who I was when I walked into my office and stop living. The compartments I'd made of 'work' and 'life' were totally artificial."

This has been a life-changing revelation for Marilyn. While she still works in advertising, she's now taking steps to change the nature of her job to something less administrative and more creative. She may even, she says, get out of the industry altogether, perhaps pursuing art—a passion of hers she'd always thought of as "self-indulgent"—maybe with a view to teaching it. "Options. That's the word. I'd felt so locked into thinking I didn't have any. Or that I had only two: either work at the job I had or be a bum and not work at all. Which also translated to: either be worth something or be worth nothing. Now, slowly, with my sponsor's and the program's help, I'm discovering that self-esteem does not come from my job. What a radical awakening *that* is! Self-esteem comes from something inside me. I can't lay it on with a brush. It has to grow from within."

What Does "Success" Mean Now?

There's an endless range of experience in recovery—from newly sober people who have lost everything and live on the street to people like Marilyn who have managed to "hold it all together," perhaps losing little in a material sense but so much in a spiritual, mental, and emotional sense. But what seems to characterize progress for all of us as we slog through whatever the external work circumstances may be in each of our lives is a new definition of "success."

We defined success at the outset of this book very simply:

You've succeeded if you've managed to keep from picking up a drink or drug today. But that definition is infinitely expandable. "Success," for so many recovering people, even in the earliest weeks and months of recovery, grows to include the sense of connection we've been exploring throughout this book. Not only that you're connected to other people but that you're a part of a whole world and universe—a spiritual sense of being important and worthy simply because you are who you are. Out of this realization (however gradually come to), we begin to feel worthy in a way that can't be injured by ego, what job we have, how much money we make, the car we drive, or the home we live in. We come to feel in some indefinable sense that we *deserve* to be loved. Even more, that we *are* loved by other people and, perhaps, even by that strange Higher Power that Twelve Step programs keep going on about.

Success happens to us in other ways, as well. We discover we're capable of accepting more from life than we ever thought we could. Recovery shows us that we can face even our worst fears, our most hateful assumptions about ourselves, without being capsized or "punished." We slowly discover a new capacity for conscious living: a humble, sometimes even awestruck state in which we begin to sift our fears and prejudices from a new, unthreatening sense of reality. We discover we don't need our old props either of mind or of behavior. We discover the amazing fact that there is, as our elderly art appraiser Charles said, a *self* waiting to appear after drinking and drugging.

Nearly all the people I've listened to who've completed their first year of sobriety have discovered something along these lines: There are wonderfully unanticipated rewards to living consciously—that is, living without losing ourselves in alcohol or drugs. Not that everything always (or even usually) gets rosy. Our pain and numbness and confusion don't always stop. We're still in uncharted territory as we finish our first sober year: day by day, moment by moment, there's the rest of our conscious lives to come. And none of us knows what's in store.

After day 365 comes day 366. You can choose to meet that new day consciously, in an attitude of sobriety. One thing we can guarantee: You don't have to face that day without help. Twelve Step programs, from the evidence of the many recovering people who follow them, can help you to deal with all the abundance of life soberly. The only advice we need to follow to prove all this to ourselves seems to come in the simple phrase, *Don't drink or drug, and go to meetings.* That, anyway, seems to be enough to open the door to the adventure of sobriety—to the discovery of just how wide your own capacity is to receive the fullest, richest measure of life.

You've Got to Give It Away to Keep It

TO:

FROM:

Suggested Reading

The following books are all official "conference-approved" publications of Alcoholics Anonymous, published by AA World Services, Inc., and are available through AA and some bookstores:

Alcoholics Anonymous (The Big Book). 3d ed. New York: Alcoholics Anonymous World Services, Inc., 1976.

Twelve Steps and Twelve Traditions. New York: Alcoholics Anonymous World Services, Inc., 1981.

As Bill Sees It. New York: Alcoholics Anonymous World Services, Inc., 1967.

Living Sober. New York: Alcoholics Anonymous World Services, Inc., 1975.

Came to Believe. New York: Alcoholics Anonymous World Services, Inc., 1973.

In addition, I heartily recommend the following:

B., Hamilton. *Getting Started in AA.* Center City, Minn.: Hazelden, 1995.

————. *Twelve Step Sponsorship: How It Works.* Center City, Minn.: Hazelden, 1996.

B., Mel. *New Wine: The Spiritual Roots of the Twelve Step Miracle.* Center City, Minn.: Hazelden, 1991.

Carnes, Patrick. *A Gentle Path through the Twelve Steps.* Center City, Minn.: Hazelden, 1993.

————. *Out of the Shadows: Understanding Sexual Addiction.* Center City, Minn.: Hazelden, 1992.

————. *Sexual Anorexia: Overcoming Sexual Self-Hatred.* Center City, Minn.: Hazelden, 1997.

Gorski, Terence T. *Passages through Recovery.* Center City, Minn.: Hazelden, 1997.

Kettelhack, Guy. *Easing the Ache: Gay Men Recovering from Compulsive Behavior.* Center City, Minn.: Hazelden, 1998.

Kominars, Sheppard B., and Kathryn D. Kominars. *Accepting Ourselves and Others: A Journey into Recovery from Addictive and Compulsive Behaviors for Gays, Lesbians and Bisexuals.* Center City, Minn.: Hazelden, 1996.

Kurtz, Ernest. *Not-God: A History of Alcoholics Anonymous.* Center City, Minn.: Hazelden, 1991.

Levine, Stephen. *A Gradual Awakening.* New York: Anchor Books, 1989.

Larsen, Earnie. *Stage II Recovery: Life Beyond Addiction.* San Francisco: HarperSanFrancisco, 1985.

————. *Stage II Relationships: Love Beyond Addiction.* San Francisco: HarperSanFrancisco, 1987.

Martin, John. *Blessed Are the Addicts: The Spiritual Side of Alcoholism, Addiction and Recovery.* New York: Villard, 1991.

Narcotics Anonymous. 5th ed. Van Nuys, Calif.: Narcotics Anonymous World Service Office, Inc., 1988.

Schaeffer, Brenda. *Is It Love or Is It Addiction?* Center City, Minn.: Hazelden, 1997.

Z., Phillip. *A Skeptic's Guide to the Twelve Steps.* Center City, Minn.: Hazelden, 1991.

About the Author

Guy Kettelhack is the author or co-author of more than a dozen nonfiction books, including

Second-Year Sobriety: Getting Comfortable Now That Everything Is Different

Third-Year Sobriety: Finding Out Who You Really Are

Easing the Ache: Gay Men Recovering from Compulsive Behaviors

Sober and Free: Making Your Recovery Work for You

On a Clear Day You Can See Yourself, with Dr. Sonya Friedman

Love Triangles, with Dr. Bonnie Jacobson

Dancing around the Volcano